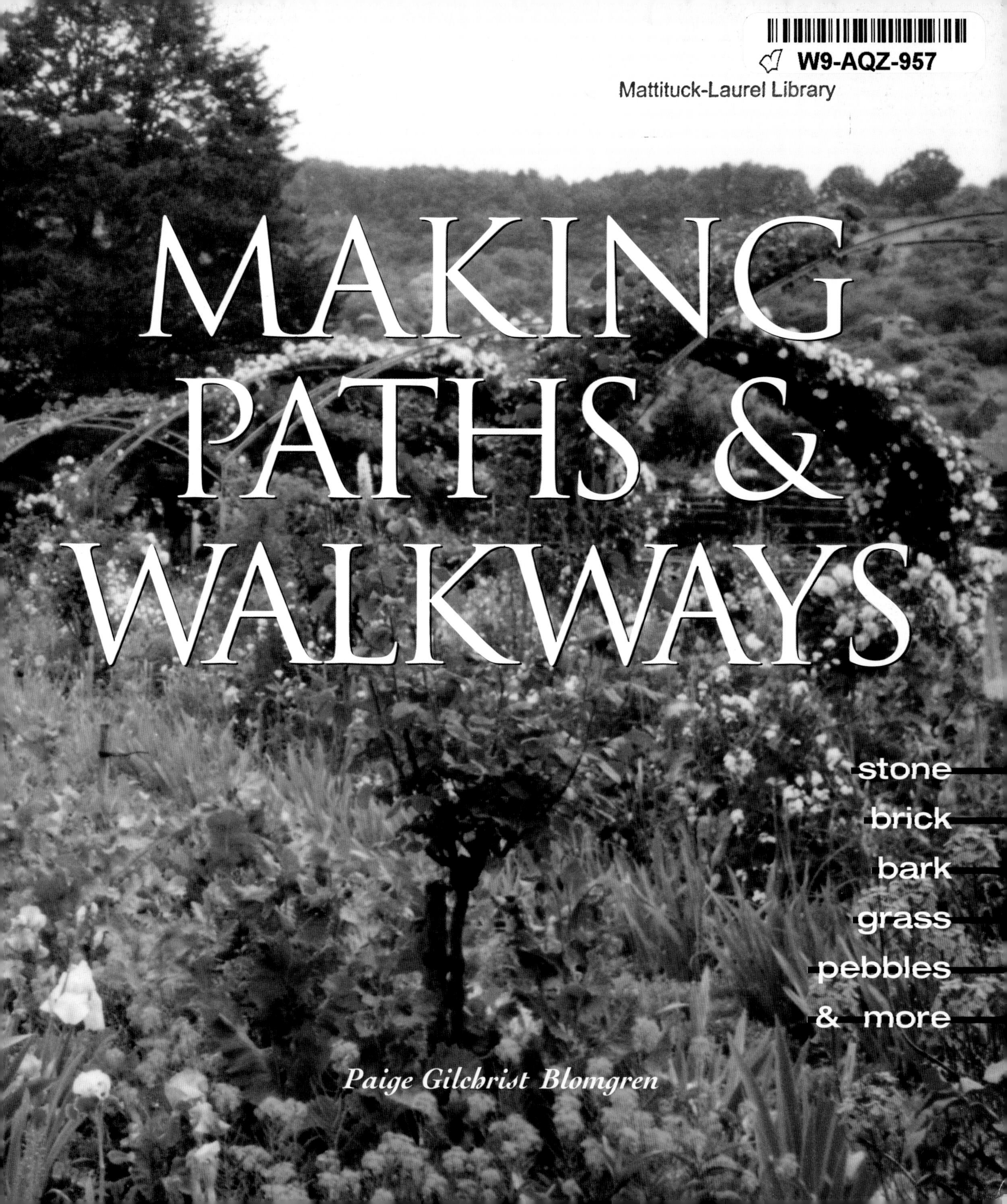

# MAKING PATHS & WALKWAYS

stone

brick

bark

grass

pebbles

& more

*Paige Gilchrist Blomgren*

CONSULTING LANDSCAPE ARCHITECT: RANDY BURROUGHS, RLA

Art Direction and Production: Celia Naranjo
Illustrations: Olivier Rollin
Chapter Opener Illustrations: Dana Irwin
Map Illustrations: Dana Irwin, Celia Naranjo, Heather Smith, Catharine Sutherland
Principal Photographer: Richard Babb
Editorial Assistance: Heather Smith and Catharine Sutherland
Production Assistance: Hannes Charen
Copy Editing: Alan H. Anderson

❧

*Preceding pages: Claude Monet's garden, Giverney, France, photograph by Dana Irwin*

Quote on page 9 is from *The Songlines* by Bruce Chatwin. Copyright © 1987 by Bruce Chatwin.
Used by permission of Viking Penguin, a division of Penguin Putnam, Inc.
Quote on page 23 from *Pilgrim at Tinker Creek* by Annie Dillard.
Copyright © 1974 by Annie Dillard. Reprinted by permission of HarperCollins Publishers, Inc.
Quote on page 39 copyright © 1946 by *The New York Times*. Reprinted by permission.
Quote on page 45 reprinted by the permission of Russell & Volkening as agents for the author.
Copyright © 1941 by Eudora Welty, renewed 1969 by Eudora Welty.
*A Worn Path* first appeared in *Atlantic Monthly*, February 1941.
Excerpt from *A Worn Path* in *A Curtain of Green and Other Stories* , copyright 1941 and renewed 1969 by Eudora Welty,
reprinted by permission of Harcourt Brace & Company.
Quote on page 61 is an excerpt from "Departure" by Edna St. Vincent Millay. From *Collected Poems*, HarperCollins.
Copyright © 1923, 1951 by Edna St. Vincent Millay and Norma Millay Ellis. All rights reserved.
Reprinted by permission of Elizabeth Barnett, literary executor.
Quotes on pages 7, 15, and 127 are in the public domain.

**Library of Congress Cataloging-in-Publication Data**

Blomgren, Paige Gilchrist.
 Making paths & walkways : stone, brick, bark, grass, pebbles & more /
Paige Gilchrist Blomgren.
  p. cm.
  Includes index.
  ISBN 1-57990-228-6
  1. Garden walks—Design and construction—Amateurs' manuals.
 I. Title.
 TH4970.B56 1999
 624—dc21       99-12166
                CIP

10 9 8 7 6 5 4 3
Published by Lark Books, a division of
Sterling Publishing Co., Inc.
387 Park Avenue South, New York, N.Y. 10016

© 2000, by Paige Gilchrist

Distributed in Canada by Sterling Publishing, c/o Canadian Manda Group, One Atlantic Ave., Suite 105, Toronto, Ontario, Canada M6K 3E7

Distributed in Australia by Capricorn Link (Australia) Pty Ltd., P.O. , Box 6651, Baulkham Hills, Business Centre, NSW 2153, Australia

Distributed in the U.K. by:, Guild of Master Craftsman Publications Ltd., Castle Place 166 High Street, Lewes, East Sussex, England, BN7 1XU
Tel: (+ 44) 1273 477374 Fax: (+ 44) 1273 478606, Email: pubs@thegmcgroup.com, Web: www.gmcpublications.com

If you have questions or comments about this book, please contact: Lark Books, 50 College St., Asheville, NC 28801, (828) 253-0467
*Printed in China*
All rights reserved
ISBN 1-57990-228-6

# TABLE OF CONTENTS

# INTRODUCTION

We long to head out, to explore new territory, change our surroundings, and find a better—or maybe just a different—view. We daydream about setting out for parts unknown as we contemplate paths to wisdom, spiritual paths, and—in the wee hours—the notion of the one true path.

At the same time, we crave order. We want our adventurous trekking (or soul-searching, as the case may be) to be accompanied by a sense of direction and structure. We're reminded of the importance of career paths, proven paths, and paths to success.

Since the earliest of times, footways have satisfied this complex set of urges, first in the form of primitive hunting and gathering tracks, later as cross-continental trade routes and spiritual odysseys. Today, as they have throughout history, paths and walkways invite us to place our feet on new ground and move forward while comfortingly showing us the way. Even if your journey extends only as far as the tool shed or the sidewalk or the rose bush, adorning your yard or garden with a path allows you to tap into an ancient and universal tradition.

The timeless pleasure of paths is that, while making your outdoor space more useful and accessible, they also make it more beautiful. In addition to providing a dry place to step while picking vegetables or a more convenient route for rolling a wheelbarrow, a path can add interest, movement, color, texture, and—most notably—individual character to your plot of land, whether you have a tiny side yard or acres in the country.

In the pages that follow, we take you down many paths: humble tracks of pine needles that wind through garden gates, classic brick walks leading to patios and porches, stepping stones that make their way through shady patches of moss—even clever concrete walks colored in every shade of the rainbow. Eight detailed sections at the heart of the book cover the procedures for making paths of materials ranging from grass and cut stone to decorative pebbles and flagstone paving. These sections are also packed with photographs to spark your imagination—and help you see where your own path might lead you.

Up front, we guide you through the steps of getting started; help you make choices about layout, materials, and design; and walk you through the tools and techniques you need for building a standard path base. You may want to follow the processes we've outlined down to the last inch of base-layer gravel. (In fact, if you're completely new to basic yard projects, you might like to pair this book with one that deals specifically with beginning landscape architecture.) If, on the other hand, you've already done your share of digging, filling, and experimenting in the yard and garden, you have likely selected this book to use more as inspiration than guide. By all means, choose your own path.

Whatever your starting point, here's a tip before you set out: Though reaching a destination (or making a path) is important, paths themselves are great reminders that the journey should be at least half the fun.

*I have met but one or two persons in the course of my life who understood the art of walking. . .who had a genius, so to speak, for sauntering.*

—Henry David Thoreau
"Walking"

# HISTORY OF
# PATHS &
# WALKWAYS

*The man who went 'Walkabout' was making
a ritual journey. He trod in the footprints
of his Ancestor. He sang the Ancestor's stanzas
without changing a word or note—
and so recreated Creation.*

~Bruce Chatwin
*The Songlines*

It's been said that if you want to plot the best route for a path, you should follow a dog—preferably an old dog. That faithful companion has likely worn the most direct and comfortable course from homeland to hunting land—or from the back door to the shady spot underneath the hammock.

For centuries, animals have traced out the world's footpaths. Their worn walks to watering holes, salt licks, and shelter were the first tried and true ways of navigating the wilderness. Early humans often adopted the primitive walkways as their own and eventually expanded them.

In many cases, animal traces evolved into traditional trails leading to gathering spots, hunting grounds, lookouts, and back to places of safety. Over time, some became wider, deeper, and linked together, providing footbeds for everything from oxcarts and horse-drawn chariots to pack animals and herds of cattle. Local paths that once connected animals and people to nearby streams or neighboring villages formed the basis for now-famous routes traveled by explorers, traders, prospectors, immigrants, homesteaders, soldiers, and groups of religious faithful seeking new lands of opportunity. Ultimately, some of these time-honored paths and trails evolved into railroad lines and modern highways.

*17th-century English walking trail leading through the fruit orchards and fields surrounding Ham Hill*

At the same time that early walking paths were being transformed into travel routes for modern civilization, the concept of the pathway was also being adapted to fit domestic needs and yearnings. Homeowners and architects began to use paths not only as practical tools for ordering outdoor environments, but also as visual elements to shape, embellish, and add beauty to gardens, yards, and public gathering places.

In some cultures, path styles that developed first to meet utilitarian needs eventually formed the foundation for popular design principles. For example, the paths of ancient Egyptian gardens were formal and orderly not because the Egyptians believed that "straighter is better," but because their paths had to follow the route of irriga-

*Formal walkway around a garden pool at the Alhambra, an Arabic palace near the base of Spain's Sierra Nevada mountains built by Moorish Kings in the 9th century*

*Formal pathways running through the front garden and hedged pathways beside water channels at a Persian palace (above and below)*

tion channels. Early Persian gardens, too, featured straight, elegant paths because they flowed best along the protective walls that separated gardens from the desolate landscape beyond. European garden designers adopted the use of symmetrical pathways, which supported their concept of imposing order on the natural world. Throughout the medieval and Renaissance periods, straight, formal paths bordering square or rectangular plant beds were the preferred style of walkway.

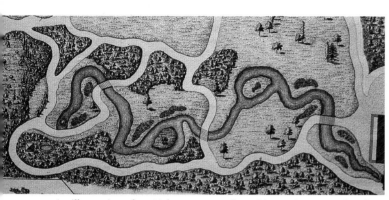

*An illustration of an 18th-century garden with curving, natural paths*

*A path venturing into the wilderness, created in the 1740s in Germany by the Margravine of Bayreuth*

In other cultures, people who created paths and walks were guided by a desire to achieve harmony with the surrounding landscape rather than to hold it at bay. In the Far East, beginning in ancient China and by around 600 A.D. in Japan and Korea, garden walks were designed not to dominate but to mimic the natural world. Natural-looking paths followed streams, wove around ponds, and simulated the rises and dips of surrounding hillsides. This approach eventually influenced the naturalistic movement in Western

*Portion of the Liberty Trail, a 17th-century trail in England's Somerset and Dorset countryside, as it winds through Wayford Woods*

*This 17th-century walkway at the Hotel Caruso Belvedere in Ravello, Italy, is framed by arches. It begins with rising steps at one end and leads to a view of the sea at the other.*

landscaping and served as an impetus for wilderness leisure trails blazed in reaction to the industrial boom.

Home path builders today can draw on this long, rich history and the wealth of path styles and designs it has inspired. The same get-away-from-it-all impulse that moved Emile Benton MacKaye at the turn of the century to imagine today's Appalachian Trail might be your own motivation to design a footpath through a stand of trees at the back of the yard. The striking monuments that flanked the Appian Way from Rome to the Mediterranean Sea could stir you to add a touch of artistry to the mundane walkway from the side door to the garage. The careful, soothing placement of stepping stones to a Japanese tea house can serve as a model for your own meditative path through the garden.

Today, the quiet allure of paths and walkways is stronger than ever as we are overwhelmed by the noise of traffic and the uniformity of interstates. Though most of us no longer need to forge a route from our place of shelter to a water source, a pleasant path that leads from the house to the garden shed can make yard work a happier task. A well-marked footpath to a lookout post is no longer a necessary part of most daily lives, but a tempting trail that invites us to a spot with a view is irresistible. Creating our own path allows us to blend beauty with utility as we adorn our out-of-doors…to combine pleasure and practicality as we make our way to that hammock where the dog is waiting.

> *Sidebars throughout this book feature some of the world's most ancient and famous paths, walkways, and trails.*

# CHAPTER TWO

# GETTING STARTED

*Afoot and light-hearted I take to the open road,*
*Healthy, free, the world before me,*
*The long brown path before me*
*leading wherever I choose.*

~Walt Whitman
"Song of the Open Road"

Should your path wind lazily along or follow a strong, straight line? Is it best to make it wide and roomy, or narrow and cozy? And how do you choose between bricks or pebbles, mulch or stepping stones? You'll be much better prepared to make these and other decisions if you start by thinking through the purpose of your path and studying the place where it will lie. Below are the key questions you should ask about purpose and place. The chapters that follow will guide you in using your answers to design your path, prepare a strong base, choose appropriate paving materials, and build the path that truly gets you where you want to go.

## PURPOSE: WHO WILL BE TRAVELING YOUR PATH, AND WHY?

Putting yourself in the place of those who will regularly use your path will help you make decisions about everything from layout to materials.

- Will your path's primary users be children with bare feet traveling from patio to pool? If so, you won't want to top it off with sharp gravel.
- Are you helping someone push a stroller to the back door or a wheelbarrow to the compost pile? Then brick or concrete will make better paving materials than decorative pebbles.
- Will a person taking out the trash regularly walk the path after dark? In that case, you'd be better off choosing a direct path of pine needles or earth rather than a meandering maze of stepping stones.

Decide whether travelers will be using your path to move efficiently from point A to point B or to take a leisurely stroll. If it's meant to be utilitarian, you'll want your path to be as direct and obstacle-free as possible.

- People juggling groceries on their way from the car to the door don't want to zigzag through a bed of perennials. In fact, they won't—they'll eventually forge a shortcut (and everyone from delivery people to guests carrying casseroles will follow).
- On the other hand, if people will be using your path to wander through your rose garden, they'll love graceful turns past trickling fountains and unexpected openings at benches and bird baths.

A utilitarian path running beside a house (left) might be much less formal, in terms of both material and design, than a main front walk (right).

Heavy-use paths designed to get people to main entrances should be wide, very comfortable underfoot, inviting, and clearly marked, whether by a gate or potted plants at the entrance or hedges along the border. A path that offers a casual tour through the herb garden might be narrower and more subtle, and a purely practical path that veers off to the tool shed may be a simple earthen track that slips off nearly unnoticed.

## PLACE: WHAT DO YOU NEED TO KNOW ABOUT YOUR PATH SITE?

### Existing Structures and Objects

Decide whether your path will abut the foundation of a house, garage, shed, or other building. If so, before laying your path base, you'll need to check (and perhaps adjust) the site's slope to make sure water is directed away from the building foundation (see Adjusting the Slope, page 46).

Also, in the early planning stages consider whether there are shapes or lines you want your path to echo, from the curve of a pool to the geometric edge of a plant bed. As outlined in Choosing Your Path Material (page 22), some path materials lend themselves better to straight walks while others are best for winding trails.

Think, too, about the style and materials of existing structures. A wide, formal brick walkway would be out of place leading to a modest cabin in the woods; a three-story estate needs something more than stepping stones for a front walk.

Finally, note whether there are nearby trees whose roots will grow and eventually cause your path to buckle (oaks and maples are notorious offenders). If so, you may want to use flexible material rather than concrete or brick as paving materials. The tree roots can crack concrete and reduce your brick walk to rubble. Other ways to deal with trees are to prune the tree roots or re-route the path.

### Climate

Think through the seasonal range of weather in your region. If you live in an area with a lot of rain or snow, prepare your path for good drainage (see Improving Drainage, page 56) or it may settle into a muddy chain of puddles. If your ground freezes hard in the winter or if your soil expands during the wet season and contracts during the dry season, a proper base is extra-important (see Laying a Base for Your Path, page 44). In Florida, the South, and southern and coastal California, on the other hand, soils are generally more stable and path bases need not be as deep.

Take climate into consideration when you select your path material as well. For example, concrete may crack and bricks may unsettle in deep freezes that cause the ground to heave; some cut stone and stepping-stone paths will be slippery when it's wet; grass paths need adequate moisture and sunlight; and tile may be too hot underfoot if it bakes in the sunshine. The Choosing Your Path Material chapter (page 22) addresses considerations like these for a full range of materials.

### Drainage

Good drainage is essential to the long-term stability of your path. By determining how well your soil drains before you begin, you'll be prepared to correct poor drainage, if necessary, when you lay your path base.

*Gravel works well as a paving material for paths on gently sloping sites.*

*Existing beds of flowers determined the layout for these natural paths.*

The makeup of your soil will give you a good idea of how well it drains. If it's sandy or gravelly, chances are water will percolate easily through it. Clay and heavy topsoil, on the other hand, hold water and may create a muddy or spongy layer beneath your path if you don't improve the drainage.

To test your soil's drainage, follow these steps:

1. Dig a hole in the path site roughly 4 inches in diameter by 12 inches deep (10 cm by 31 cm) and fill it with water.

2. Let the hole drain, then refill it.

3. If it doesn't drain again within 12 hours, your soil's drainage is poor. You can improve it by excavating the path base at the deepest level suggested for the path type you're building and by laying a drainage pipe in your base (see Improving Drainage, page 56).

It's also important to know how water naturally drains on the site you've chosen for your path. Go outside during a heavy rain and study the movement of storm water across the ground. Or, if you'd rather stay dry, sprinkle a line of lime, pine bark chips, or anything else that will float down the center of your path site. After a rain, the material will show the water run-off pattern. When you prepare the ground for your path, you'll want to take advantage of natural drainage to direct water off and away from the path or to carry water along the run of the path and toward an existing drainage area.

## Terrain

If the path site slopes steeply, consider how you'll adjust it to accommodate your path (see Adjusting the Slope, page 46). The terrain should also guide your choice of materials. Certain materials are better for paths that slope. Gravel, for instance, is less likely than mulch to wash downslope in a heavy rain, and it won't be as slippery as slate pavers when it's wet. Also, with a sloped path you'll want to take precautions against leaving low spots where puddles form.

## Available Materials

Ask local suppliers (and other path builders) about paving materials that are available in your area. Are there native stones? Are pine needles so common that they are baled for sale each year? Is there a source of river gravel? Heavy paving materials, such as brick, stone, and ornamental gravel, are costly to transport, making local materials not only better suited to your climate, but also less expensive.

*Native stone and other local materials will be much less expensive and more readily available than those that must be transported.*

## PERSONAL INVESTMENT: HOW MUCH TIME, EFFORT, AND MONEY DO YOU WANT TO SPEND?

Finally, before you order a load of paving materials and start digging, give some thought to the magnitude of the project you are willing to take on. Laying down a short stepping-stone path from the back door to the tomato plants will be a considerably easier undertaking than building a concrete front walk with embedded tile designs. A casual garden path topped with straw will be far less expensive than an ornate, cut-stone promenade. Study the Choosing Your Path Material chapter (page 22), which outlines everything from purchasing information to difficulty of construction for a range of materials. The sections in Chapter Six that tell you how to lay various types of paths will also help you gauge how involved a project you have in mind might be.

# CHAPTER THREE

# CHOOSING YOUR PATH MATERIAL

*We must somehow take a wider view, look at the whole landscape, really see it, and describe what's going on here. Then we can at least wail the right question into the swaddling band of darkness or, if it comes to that, choir the proper praise.*

~Annie Dillard
*Pilgrim at Tinker Creek*

Every paving material has its pros and cons—characteristics you'll want to consider before deciding which one to use. In this chapter, we provide overviews of common paving materials so you can compare, contrast, and determine which one is best for the path you want to build.

## Natural Material

**EFFECT ACHIEVED:**

Materials such as pine needles, bark mulches, straw, crushed shells, and earth create the most informal, natural-looking paths.

**ADVANTAGES:**

Natural material paths are among the least expensive and easiest to build, and they conform easily to areas with slight dips, rises, and curves.

**DISADVANTAGES:**

Natural material paths can become soggy and can break down or erode quickly. Weeds can invade them, and the materials can be tracked to inside environments if the path is near the house. All organic materials break down and need periodic refreshing, depending on climate and use. Bark and needles tend to wash away when it rains on sloping sites.

**CLIMATE CONSIDERATIONS:**

Specific materials such as pine needles may be readily available only in certain regions. Natural material paths in rainy areas might become too boggy. In windy areas, materials might blow away, and in most areas they are susceptible to invasion by weeds.

**DURABILITY:**

Varies. Dirt has good durability, unless the area becomes too muddy. Pine needles, bark mulches, and straw have poor durability under heavy use.

**DIFFICULTY OF CONSTRUCTION:**

Easy.

**CALCULATING QUANTITY:**

Multiply the length and width of your path by the depth you want for your surface layer to determine the volume of material needed. This will give you cubic feet or meters. Divide by 27 to convert cubic feet to cubic yards. Natural materials may be sold by the truck load or the bale—in bulk by the cubic yard and in bags by the cubic foot. Sellers will be happy to help you determine the amount you need, based on the area to be covered. For example, one bale of pine needles covers 40 square feet (12.3 square meters) to a depth of 3 to 4 inches (8 to 10 cm). For small projects, pine bark nuggets can be bought by the bag at home and building supply stores; refer to the bag for recommended coverage. Shredded hardwood bark is usually sold in bulk by the cubic yard (1 cubic yard of shredded hardwood usually covers 81 square feet 3 inches deep [25 square meters 8 cm deep]). It knits together well and doesn't erode as easily as pine bark, and it's more durable. A bare soil garden path is made by use—the worn path—but may need some grading or stepping stones to keep it from becoming muddy.

**WHERE TO PURCHASE:**

Some materials you can collect yourself in the woods or other areas. Others can be purchased from garden centers, saw mills, farms, and other suppliers of regional materials. Bulk suppliers will generally load your truck for free or deliver for a small fee.

**PRICING:**

Most natural materials are priced by the cubic foot or meter and sold in bags. Or, they're priced in bulk and sold by the bale at home, garden, or building supply stores. The cost is relatively low; a natural material path is typically the least expensive type you can build.

# Gravel & Ornamental Stone

**EFFECT ACHIEVED:**

Gravel, crushed stone, and decorative pebbles add ribbons of texture, color, and sound (that nice crunching underfoot) to both formal and informal areas.

**ADVANTAGES:**

Gravel paths are among the least expensive path types you can build. If properly graded, they drain quickly, hold well on moderate slopes, and retain their shape if the ground heaves.

**DISADVANTAGES:**

Gravel paths can wash on steep slopes and weeds can invade them. The pebbly materials can also be tracked inside if the path is near a door, and gravel tracked onto stone or brick steps or patios can roll underfoot.

**CLIMATE CONSIDERATIONS:**

Grade for a cross slope or prepare a draining base if you're working in a wet climate.

**DURABILITY:**

Good. You may need to occasionally rake spillage back onto the path and replenish the gravel.

**DIFFICULTY OF CONSTRUCTION:**

Moderate.

**CALCULATING QUANTITY:**

Most bags of loose rock materials are sold by the cubic foot, while bulk purchases are usually made in cubic yards or tons. To calculate materials in cubic feet or meters, multiply the width and length of the path by the desired depth of the material, keeping all measurements in feet or meters. Divide cubic feet by 27 to convert to cubic yards.

**WHERE TO PURCHASE:**

Gravel and other loose rock paving materials can be purchased from sand and gravel suppliers, who sell by the cubic yard or the ton. You can cart loose rock and gravel home in a pick-up truck or have your order delivered for a fee. Gravel or stone any larger than ¾ inch (2 cm) can be difficult to walk on. For best results, select ⅜-inch stones (1 cm).

**PRICING:**

You'll get the best pricing on the quantity of loose rock usually needed to fill a path or walkway by buying in bulk at a quarry, a sand and gravel yard, or at another stone supplier. Bulk suppliers sell gravel and loose rock by the ton (2000 pounds or 907 kilograms). For smaller projects, bags of pebbles are available at home, garden, and building supply stores. Decorative stones are more expensive than pea gravel. A simple gravel path costs about the same or slightly more than a natural material path.

# Grass

**EFFECT ACHIEVED:**

These strips of natural green can be formal or informal, and they present handsome foregrounds for flower beds, herbaceous borders, and shrub gardens.

**ADVANTAGES:**

Grass paths are cool under bare feet, they work well on sloping land, and they're among the least expensive paths you can build.

**DISADVANTAGES:**

Keeping a grass path green may be a challenge in drought-prone areas. If you're creating a grass path from seed rather than sod, you'll have to refrain from walking on it for several weeks after sowing the seeds. Weeds can be a problem, and newly seeded soil can erode on sloped areas. Excess traffic can wear bald spots in the path. Oh, and you'll be doing some mowing.

*Sod being cut at a sod farm.*

**CLIMATE CONSIDERATIONS:**

Grass paths do best in full sun, need plenty of water, and can turn to mud in snowy winter climates. Warm season grasses (Bermuda, zoysia, centipede) endure traffic best, but they go dormant in winter. (They do best in climate zones 8 and higher.) Cool season grasses (fescue, bluegrass, rye) are evergreen, but often need overseeding to stay thick. Use red fescue in areas of heavy shade.

**DURABILITY:**

Fair to good, depending on maintenance and traffic.

**DIFFICULTY OF CONSTRUCTION:**

Moderate in good soil, though laying sod is heavy work.

**CALCULATING QUANTITY:**

Sod is sold by the pallet and comes in strips 18 to 24 inches (46 to 62 cm) wide and 2 to 5 feet (.6 to 1.5 m) long. Grass seed is typically pre-bagged and sold by the pound at garden centers, where retailers can guide you on how much you need to cover your path. Note that seed sizes vary; for example, 5 to 6 pounds (2 kilograms) of fescue seed will cover the same 1000-square-foot (307-square-meter) area as 2 to 3 pounds (1 kilogram) of Bermuda seed. Multiply the length of your path by the width to get the total square feet or meters you need to cover with seed.

**WHERE TO PURCHASE:**

Sod can be purchased directly from a sod farm, which is typically less expensive than a garden center. If purchasing from a sod grower, calculate the square yardage of the area and order your sod in advance so it can be cut before you arrive. Most sod companies deliver for an extra charge for minimum orders of 4 pallets, or 240 square yards (200 square meters).

**PRICING:**

Sod strips are priced by the square yard. Seed costs vary according to type and from year to year, but seed will be a fraction of the cost of sod.

# Cut Stone

Cut stone refers to any stone paving material that has been cut into a uniform shape, usually a square or rectangle ranging in size from about 1 square foot to 4 square feet (.3 square m to 1.2 square m). Types of cut stone will vary by region and include limestone, sandstone, bluestone, slate, and granite.

**EFFECT ACHIEVED:**

Cut stone provides a formal, stately look.

**ADVANTAGES:**

Especially handsome (and formal) when laid in mortar on a cement base. Large stones on a flexible base are striking, too. Cut stone is nearly permanent and can provide a smooth surface.

**DISADVANTAGES:**

Slate and marble pavers are very smooth and become slick when wet. They're especially dangerous when used for sloping walks or ramps.

**CLIMATE CONSIDERATIONS:**

Cut stone can be susceptible to cracking in harsh winter climates.

**DURABILITY:**

Excellent, though limestone will wear down with years of weathering and use.

**DIFFICULTY OF CONSTRUCTION:**

A cut stone walkway is one of the most labor-intensive path types. However, cut stones may also be placed informally to form simple stepping-stone paths.

**CALCULATING QUANTITY:**

Multiply the length of your path by its width to get the square feet or meters of stone needed.

**WHERE TO PURCHASE:**

Purchase from masonry suppliers, stone yards, and tile companies. Cut stones can be transported in a pick-up truck or delivered to your site for a fee (many suppliers charge a flat local delivery rate and sometimes add mileage costs, depending on the distance.)

**PRICING:**

Cut stone is sold by the square foot or meter, and prices vary by size and color. Cut stone is more expensive than most materials, with rare colors such as desert rose or oak being the most costly.

# Natural Stone

Naturally-occurring or quarried flat stones of various sizes, colors, shapes, and thicknesses make charming paths that are less formal looking than cut stone paths. Fieldstone, collected from fields or old stone walls, is often rough and weathered. Quarried stone, dynamited or pried from large rock masses in the earth, can have a cleaner look. Common types of quarried stone include sandstone, granite, and limestone. Large, 3- to 4-inch-thick (8-10 cm) pieces make the most stable paths.

### EFFECT ACHIEVED:

The random shapes and aged surfaces of natural stone create a rustic, informal look. Natural stones also lend themselves to imaginative patterns, and their irregular gaps leave perfect spots for planting. Some have very attractive colors.

### ADVANTAGES:

Stone walks can be laid on level and gently sloping surfaces, and the stones can be broken and shaped for a good fit. Locally available materials can often be used to build a stone pathway.

### DISADVANTAGES:

Stones with irregular surfaces will collect puddles when it rains.

### CLIMATE CONSIDERATIONS:

Puddles that collect on the surface of concave stones will form pools of ice in winter climates. Small, dry-laid stones will be subject to frost heave in cold winters. Poorly mixed or thin mortar joints between natural stones will tend to crumble.

### DURABILITY:

Good to excellent.

### DIFFICULTY OF CONSTRUCTION:

Laying stone is a bit like doing a very heavy jigsaw puzzle. Every piece is different, so you may end up spending a good deal of time fitting each to your liking. Simply laying stones one after the other in a stepping-stone fashion is far less labor-intensive.

### CALCULATING QUANTITY:

Multiply the length of the path by the width to get square feet or meters needed. Though stone is generally sold by the ton, the square foot or meter figure will allow your supplier to roughly calculate the amount needed.

### WHERE TO PURCHASE:

If you don't have access to fieldstones, purchase flagstone from stone yards. They will load your truck or car with small amounts. Delivery costs extra and depends on the size of the truck and the distance.

**PRICING:**

Because stone is sold by the ton, prices vary greatly according to the thickness and type of stone. Other factors affect price, too. Some colors are more expensive than others. Fieldstone, which is labor-intensive to gather, is more costly than quarried stone. And you'll pay more if you want to hand-pick your stones at a quarry.

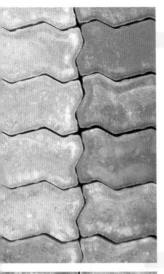

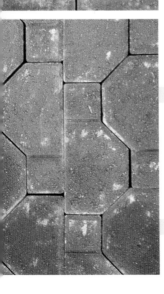

# Brick

**EFFECT ACHIEVED:**

Because bricks come in various colors and textures and can be combined in many different patterns, they can be used to create everything from regal walkways to homey paths with plant- or moss-filled gaps. Be sure to use paving bricks rather than facing bricks, which are intended for walls.

**ADVANTAGES:**

Their standard size makes bricks easy to quantify and to lay. They usually mix well with other materials. For example, brick makes an excellent edging for gravel paths.

**DISADVANTAGES:**

Growing tree roots can cause brick paths to buckle. Batches of bricks can be difficult to match if you're trying to connect a new walk to an existing structure, such as a patio. Also, old brick, which looks charming, may not hold up well.

**CLIMATE CONSIDERATIONS:**

Old bricks may crack or crumble in winter climates. Bricks tend to grow mossy and slick in rainy climates, and to get hot underfoot in sunny areas.

**DURABILITY:**

Good, depending on the quality; old brick doesn't weather well.

**DIFFICULTY OF CONSTRUCTION:**

Requires great attention to detail, especially if you're laying intricate patterns, and needs a firm base to maintain a smooth surface.

**CALCULATING QUANTITY:**

Brick pavers are typically 2 inches thick, 3½ inches wide, and 7¾ inches long (5 cm by 8.75 cm by 19.4 cm). It takes approximately five bricks to pave a square foot (.3 square m). Multiply the length of your path by the width to get the total square feet or meters (the area). Keep in mind that bricks come in different sizes—brick pavers come in thin or thick shapes (1 inch to 2 inches, or 2.5 cm to 5 cm)—and brick laid on edge will cover less area.

**WHERE TO PURCHASE:**

Bricks can be purchased through brick suppliers, tile companies, and home and building supply centers. A full-sized pick-up truck with good suspension can normally haul about 1000 pounds (450 kilograms) or more of bricks, but most suppliers will deliver for a fee. Renting a load-and-go vehicle is another option available at some home and building suppliers—they load the vehicle, you drive it home and unload it.

**PRICING:**

Bricks are sold individually, so the cost will depend on how many bricks you need and what style of brick you choose. The three common colors of brick—red, tan, and gray—sell for the same price, but the price of brick in other styles and other colors may vary.

# CONCRETE

### EFFECT ACHIEVED:

Because of concrete's versatility, it can be used to achieve almost any effect. It can be poured into curved forms or symmetrical molds to make pavers; it can be colored; it can be stamped with brick or rock patterns; or it can be decorated with embedded materials, such as pebbles, shells, brick, and crushed tile. Concrete can also be textured with brooms, leaf imprints, or burlap, and different floats can be used to vary the smoothness.

### ADVANTAGES:

Usually needs no base. Durable and easy to clean.

*Concrete pavers provide an alternative to pouring a concrete path. Calculate quantity as you would for cut stone.*

### DISADVANTAGES:

A bit tricky for beginners, and unforgiving of mistakes. It loses durability if it's mixed too long. Once the concrete has hardened, chances are you'll have to break your path to pieces and start over if you want to make changes. And it may be hard to match patchwork to the original.

### CLIMATE CONSIDERATIONS:

Harsh winter climates and growing tree roots can cause concrete to crack. It gets hot underfoot in summer and cold and icy in winter.

### DURABILITY:

Good, if mixed and poured correctly.

### DIFFICULTY OF CONSTRUCTION:

Concrete paths require more careful planning and more equipment than other path types. A concrete path should be poured in sections that can be finished before the concrete sets. Expansion joints are needed every 12 feet (4 m) and at abutments to existing buildings or patios. Extremes of heat and cold can cause damage during concrete "curing."

### CALCULATING QUANTITY:

Generally, a bag of pre-mixed concrete (to which you add only water) will say how much coverage it will provide. Multiply the length by the width and depth of the walkway to determine how many bags you will need. For a concrete path 20 feet long, 4 inches thick and 4 feet wide (6.5 m long, 10 cm thick, and 1.2 m wide), buy materials for approximately 29 cubic feet of concrete (20 x .33 x 4, plus 10 percent for spillage or waste) or .8 m³. Divide by 27 to convert cubic feet to cubic yards, and you get just over 1 cubic yard. For large jobs, buy in bulk (Portland cement, sand, and aggregate) and rent a power cement mixer, or order ready-to-pour concrete by the cubic yard.

**WHERE TO PURCHASE:**

Bags of concrete can be purchased at home and building supply centers. Most will deliver for a fee.

**PRICING:**

Concrete mix is priced per bag (with bags usually weighing about 60 pounds or 27 kilograms). A walkway that measures 48 square feet or 15 square meters and 4 inches (10 cm) deep will require approximately 32 bags of concrete mix.

# CHAPTER FOUR

# TOOLS & EQUIPMENT

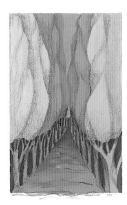

*All walking is discovery. On foot we take time to see things whole. We see trees as well as forests, people as well as crowds. When the mood is right—and walking provokes such a mood when we are most in need of it— we can even see ourselves with particular clarity. We get our feet back on the ground.*

~Hal Borland
"To Own the Streets and Fields."
*New York Times Magazine, October 6, 1946*

The basic list of tools and equipment needed to make a path is surprisingly brief. If you spend time digging in the garden and/or doing easy projects around the house and yard, chances are you already have much of what's required. You can probably borrow anything you're missing, or purchase what you need for a modest price. In a few cases we recommend that you rent non-standard items; these are easy to find at a local equipment rental service. Also, at the beginning of each section on specific kinds of paths (starting on page 60) there's a short list of additional tools or pieces of equipment you might need for that project. Once you begin using the tools, you'll gain a feel for how to make substitutions (you might be more comfortable with a different digging tool than the one we've recommended, for example) and where to add to the list (it's common to have favorite tools for specific jobs).

## General Tools & Equipment

- **4-foot (1.2 m) level and/or string level.** Levels are essential for building a path. You'll use them when you first grade your site, when you set the final paving stones in place, and at several stages in between. Techniques for using levels are described in detail beginning on page 47.

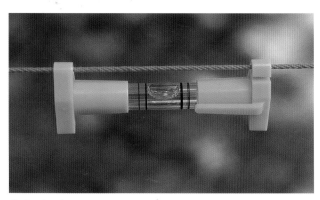

*String level*

- **Screed.** You'll want to make this special leveling tool (which you drag over base or surface materials) yourself so the size is exactly right. Simply cut notches out of a 2x6-inch [5x15-cm] board so it fits over your path edging and can be used to level the material underneath it.

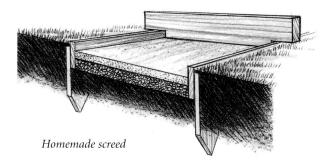

*Homemade screed*

- **Hard iron rake.** A rake is handy for spreading piles of gravel, sand, or decorative stone.
- **Trowels.** A pointing trowel is best for mortaring brick and stone; a finishing trowel works for smoothing surfaces.

*Pointing trowel and finishing trowel*

- **Wheelbarrow.** You'll need a wheelbarrow for hauling out dirt and hauling in materials to fill the path.

- **Tamping tool.** As you make your path, you'll need to compact the layers. Hand tampers with metal plates typically measure 8 inches by 8 inches (20 by 20 cm) or 10 inches by 10 inches (26 by 26 cm) and are available at supply stores. Or, you can make your own tamper by nailing a solid, 8-inch-square (20-cm-square) piece of thick lumber to one end of a 5-foot-long (1.5 m) 4x4-inch (10x10-cm) piece of lumber (or any similar scrap material you can find). For a large site (200 square feet [18.6 m²] or more), you may want to rent a drum roller you can fill with water.

*200-pound (90 kilogram) drum roller*

- **Hammer, saw, and heavy-duty work gloves.** These standbys will come in handy for a variety of activities, from cutting and pounding stakes to cutting drainpipe to carrying rough paving materials.

## Tools for Laying Out Your Path

- **Pin flags and inverted marking paint.** The easiest way to lay out a path is to use pin flags and inverted marking paint. Tying string between wooden stakes is another option. For a curving path, you might want to experiment with the layout first using a hose or a rope, then mark the borders with pin flags or stakes.

*Pin flags, measuring tape, inverted marking paint, level*

*A path site layed out with pin flags and marking paint.*

## Digging Tools

- **Mattock.** A mattock has a broad, slightly curved digging blade at one end and a small, chopping blade or pick at the other, making one end useful for loosening packed earth and embedded rocks and the other just right for cutting out roots.

- **Square-bladed shovel.** Square-bladed shovels are good for leveling rough spots, skimming grass, and later scooping gravel to fill the path base.

- **Round-nose shovel.** This all-purpose tool is helpful for digging and for spreading material into the path base.

- **Lopping shears or pruning saw.** If you need to cut back small roots, these will come in handy; for larger roots you'll need an axe.

- **Foot adz hoe.** This tool is preferred for some digging jobs and perfect for skimming a layer of grass off the surface grade or for breaking up clay.

*Metal tamp, mattocks, foot adz hoe, shovels, metal rake*

## Equipment for Laying the Base

- **Landscape fabric.** A protective layer can help retard the growth of weeds through your path and keep sediment from seeping into a perforated drainpipe.

- **4-inch (10-cm) perforated drainpipe.** This plastic pipe, used in a path base to improve drainage, is sold at home and building supply centers in various lengths that you can shorten with a saw or lengthen by joining pieces together. Sometimes, the pipe is already fitted with a "sock" that prevents sediment from seeping in. Other times you may have to purchase the sock separately and fit it around the pipe yourself.

*Landscape fabric, pipe sock, perforated drainage pipe*

## Finishing Tools

- **Broom.** A broom is helpful for sweeping sand into cracks and cleaning up.

- **Rubber mallet.** This tool can be used for tapping paving stones or brick into place.

- **Length of rebar.** Use a length of rebar as a pry bar when rearranging paving material.

- **Stone mason's hammer.** With a head that is broad and flat at one end and tapers to a wedge at the other, a stone mason's hammer is just right for breaking and trimming stone.

*Stone mason's hammer, rubber mallet, rebar, broom*

# LAYING A BASE FOR YOUR PATH

*"Walk pretty," she said. "This the easy place.
This the easy going."*

~Eudora Welty
*A Worn Path*

Though you may think first of surface materials such as pebbles and wood chips when you picture a path, the unseen, unheralded layer underneath is what keeps a path stable and firm. To lay a standard, flexible (as opposed to concrete) path base, simply follow the procedures and how-to photos in this chapter. With certain paving materials, the base "recipe" will change slightly. Those changes are explained within the individual sections on making paths, beginning on page 60.

We've also included details for pouring a concrete base, beginning on page 53. This alternative is more labor intensive and more expensive than a standard, flexible base, but it provides a more solid, durable foundation, which you may want if you're building a brick or stone path. You can dry-lay brick or stone in sand on a concrete base or, for maximum durability, you can mortar the materials into place on a thin layer of wet cement.

### Clearing and Smoothing the Ground

Clear your path site by removing any stumps, old concrete, or sod. If you're building a path on a completely flat surface, you'll have little smoothing to do. Likewise, if the ground gently rises and falls and you're planning a path of grass, stepping stones, or loose materials such as gravel or wood chips, your path can follow the contours of the land with little problem. Your job might be as simple as leveling prominent bumps and filling potholes.

If you intend to lay a path of stone, concrete, or brick on an uneven or undulating area, however, you'll need to smooth the ground first. To do so, use a mattock to loosen the earth, a square-blade shovel to skim off soil from high spots, and a wheelbarrow to carry soil to places you need to build up. When filling in deep areas, add soil in 6-inch (15-cm) layers and compact it well using a hand-held tamping tool. If your site is 200 square feet (18.6 m²) or more, you may want to rent a gasoline-powered tamper (and purchase a set of earplugs to wear when using it!).

### Adjusting the Slope

When you're laying out your path, study the way it slopes. If the slope is gentle, take advantage of it to help direct water off or away from the path surface. If it's too steep to walk on comfortably, you'll want to adjust the slope, with options ranging from cutting the path across the slope to building in landings and/or steps. (A brief description of adding steps to a path appears on page 49. For more complicated situations you may want to consult a landscape architect or builder.)

## WHAT PERCENTAGE OF SLOPE TELLS YOU

| | |
|---|---|
| 0%–1.5% | The site is fairly flat and will need cross-slope drainage or drainage through the walk surface to get rid of standing rain water. |
| 1.5%–5% | The site is prime walk slope. |
| 5%–8% | The site is technically considered a "ramp," and you should consider adding steps or even a handrail. |
| 8%–15% | The site is steep. Mulches and gravel will wash, and your path will be slippery when it's icy. |

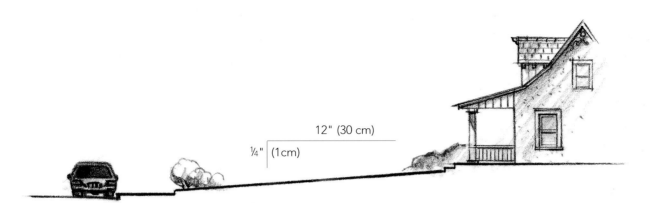

*Figure 1. A two-percent slope*

House sites should already be graded to direct water away from the foundation; make sure your path takes advantage of this slope, especially if it abuts the foundation of the house (such as a path that meets the front door) or if it runs alongside the house or another structure. For example, a path from the front door to the street should slope away from the house at ¼ inch per foot (1 cm per 30 cm) for a two-percent slope (see Figure 1). A path running parallel to a tool shed might slope the same percentage, but do so across its width (a cross slope) (see Figure 2). A standard two-percent slope is nearly imperceptible to a

walker, but it's enough to direct water off the path and away from buildings.

To monitor the slope of a path site as you're grading it, use a level that has double lines on the level's vial; a 4-foot-long (1.2 m) model is most useful. First, set it on any level surface, then lift up one end to the slope position you're trying to achieve. Say, for example, you want a two-percent slope. With a 4-foot-long level, lift one end 1 inch (3 cm); raise a 2-foot-long (61 cm) level ½ inch (1.5 cm). With the level supported in this position, the air bubble inside should rest against the outer line on the level's vial, which marks a two-percent slope. As you grade the site, periodically rest the level on the ground and adjust the soil, as necessary, to maintain a two-percent slope.

For long runs of path, you may want to use a string level. You can use it to determine the slope of your entire path site, so you know whether you need to add or remove soil from certain areas to improve drainage.

Here's how. A string level attaches to the middle of a taut string tied to two stakes, one at the high end of

*Figure 2. A two-percent cross slope (illustration not to scale)*

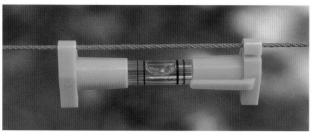
*Figure 3*

your path (at the door of the house, for example), the other at the low end. To determine the slope of such a run or a section of a run, adjust the string until the air bubble rests in the center of the vial, meaning the string is level (see Figure 3). (It's best to have someone help you with this, so one person can watch the air bubble while the other adjusts the string.) Once the string is level, measure the distance from string to ground at each end of your path (or at each end of the section for which you're determining the slope). Calculate the difference between those two measurements, and divide that number by the length of your path or of the section you're working with. The result-

ing figure is your percentage of slope. Say, for example, you have a 50-foot (15 m) path. The distance from string to ground at one end is 1 foot (.3 m); at the other end it's 2 feet (.6 m). Divide the difference (1 foot or .3 m) by the length of the path (50 feet or 15 m) and you get .02, or two percent. This means your path has a two-percent slope (see Figure 4).

If you plan to build your path on a steeper slope, keep in mind that a rise or descent of any more than 1 foot in 12 feet of path (.3 m over 3.6 m) is generally too steep for comfortable walking over much distance. To grade a slope that is steeper than that, lay your path out so that it weaves back and forth across the slope, or add steps at various intervals.

## Laying Out Your Path

Use pin flags (available at home and building supply centers and some hardware stores) or stakes every two paces (approximately 6 feet or 1.8 m) to define the

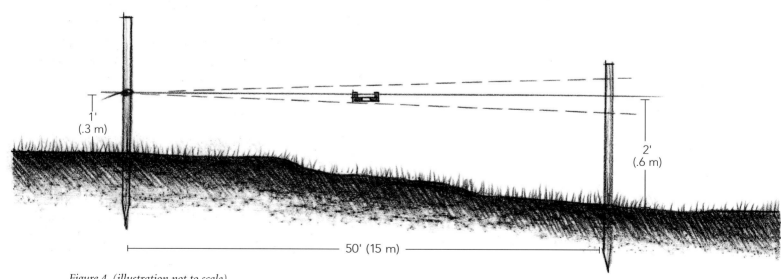

1'
(.3 m)

2'
(.6 m)

50' (15 m)

*Figure 4. (illustration not to scale)*

borders of your path, then spray the borders with inverted marking paint (see Figure 5). Garden hoses or rope can be used to lay out a path that winds and curves. Once you're satisfied with the design, leave the hose or rope in place and set pin flags or stakes—again, every two paces—to mark the edges, then remove the hose or rope and spray the outline.

*Figure 5*

Don't forget to make sure the width of your path remains constant. The standard walking-surface width for a path is 2 feet (.6 m) per person, so if you want your path to accommodate two people walking side by side, plan for it to be a minimum of 4 feet (1.2 m) wide. For one person plus an object (such as a wheelbarrow or a trash can), the standard width is 3 feet (.9 m). If you plan to hollow out space in the base for edging, add the necessary inches (depending on the thickness of your edging material) to your path width before marking it.

# WHEN YOU NEED A STEP UP (OR DOWN)

If your path must cross a steep area, you may want to simply add a few steps rather than doing a lot of digging to alter the slope. Here's an easy way to make spaced-landing timber steps. First, clear the step area of plants, leaves, and topsoil. Then, measure the distance in height between the spots where you want the top and bottom steps. Divide the measurement by the step height (the width of your timbers) to get the number of steps you need. Space your timbers evenly, working from the bottom of the slope to the top, compacting the soil behind each timber as you go. Before anchoring the timbers, walk the steps to make sure the layout is comfortable. Finally, drill two ⅝-inch (1.5-cm) holes through the center of each timber about 6 inches (15 cm) in from each end. Drive 24-inch (62-cm) pieces of #5 rebar down through the holes into the ground below until they're flush with the top of the timber. For another version of informal steps, you can place pieces of natural stone at similar intervals. If you're interested in more elaborate steps, *The Art and Craft of Stonescaping,* by David Reed (Lark Books, 1998) provides a thorough overview of stone steps and terraces. In addition, numerous gardening and landscaping books cover step building in detail.

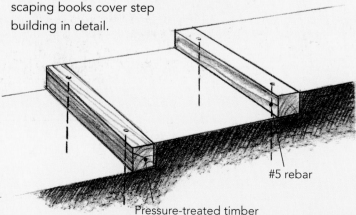

#5 rebar

Pressure-treated timber

*Figure 6*

*Figure 7*

*Figure 8*

If you are building the path into a steep slope and plan to add steps to portions of the route, mark off that area at this stage or when you dig out the path base.

## Digging Out the Base

You'll need to hollow out a trench approximately 6 to 7 inches (15 to 18 cm) deep to hold your path (depending on the thickness of your paving material). Plus, if you plan to add edging, you should dig out "shelves" for the edging at this point as well (see Edging, page 58). Increase the depth of your base by 4 inches (10 cm) if you also plan to add a drainage pipe (see Improving Drainage, page 56) and/or if you live in a climate where hard freezes are common or where the soil expands during a wet season.

A mattock or a foot adz hoe is good for loosening and carving out packed earth, removing rocks that are embedded in the ground, and cutting out small roots (see Figure 6). Use a shovel to toss your loosened soil into a wheelbarrow and, at the same time, to smooth the sides of the trench and edging shelves and to level the bottom (see Figure 7). You may use some of the soil to level the base. The rest you can move to a storage spot and use later to fill low spots in the lawn, transplant plants, or build up the compost pile. Use a level to check the slope of your base as you work (see Figure 8).

## Adding Materials for a Standard Path Base

**1.** Fill your hollowed-out trench with 3 inches (8 cm) of ½-inch to ¾-inch (1.5-cm to 2-cm) washed gravel (see Figure 9) and use a shovel to level it (or to achieve a two-percent cross slope if you're sloping the path for drainage; see Improving Drainage, page 56). Walk back and forth over this gravel layer to pack it down (a lawn roller or big-footed friends would be helpful here). If you're working on a slope, begin at the low end and work your way up so you keep packing the base materials firmly against each other as you go.

*Figure 9*

Alternative: If drainage is not a problem at your path site, you may want to substitute "crusher run" gravel (also known as "road bond") for washed gravel. Because it compacts so well, this inexpensive material, commonly used in road building, has the character of a fixed, solid base (almost like concrete), yet it's still flexible enough to accommodate shifts underneath the path, such as growing tree roots. A word of caution: this base is so stable that it doesn't allow water to drain quickly through it. If you need good drainage, stick with washed gravel for this base layer.

*Figure 10*

**2.** Next, you may want to lay a landscape cloth to filter sediment out of draining storm water and to serve as a weed barrier. (A landscape cloth isn't necessary to filter sediment if you've used crusher run instead of gravel in your base.) You can purchase landscape cloth at garden centers in 3-, 4-, and 6-foot (.9-, 1.2-, and 1.8-m) widths and cut it with scissors. (Make sure you get cloth wide enough to both cover your path and to be held in place under your edging stones if you're using them [see Figure 10].) Non-woven landscape cloth is best; it's not as slick as the woven cloth, and it doesn't break down as quickly.

*Figure 11*

*Figure 12*

*Figure 13*

**3.** Finish your base by smoothing in a 1-inch (3-cm) settling bed of sand (see Figure 11). This leaves several inches for paving materials. (Your finished surface should be slightly above the surrounding ground.) Be sure to check the level of your path base at this final stage (see Figure 12 ).

**4.** At this point, the base is ready, and you can begin laying the paving material (see Figure 13).

Figure 14 shows a cross-section of a standard, flexible path base.

### ORDERING BASE MATERIALS

You can order base materials from a sand and gravel yard. To figure out how much you'll need, there are two different formulas.

**1.** When figuring the amount of sand or gravel to cover the width and length of the path, multiply the length of the path times its width, and multiply the result by the depth of the sand or gravel (in feet or meters). This will give you the amount you need in cubic feet (or cubic meters). Divide the number of cubic feet by 27 to determine how many cubic yards you need. Sand and gravel suppliers typically sell by the cubic yard, cubic foot (or cubic meter), or the ton, and they'll be glad to help you calculate the amount you need.

**Example: Calculating amount of sand needed.**
Path length: 30 feet (9 m)
Path width: 4 feet (1.2 m)
Sand depth: 1 inch or .08 feet (.02 m)
30 x 4 x .08 = 9.6 cubic feet (or .27 m³)

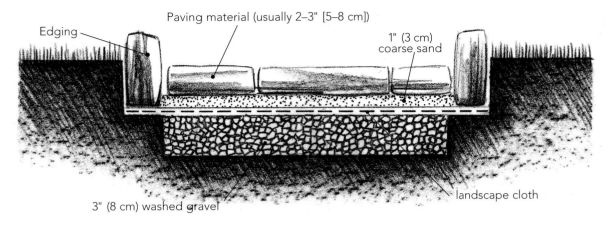

Edging

Paving material (usually 2–3" [5–8 cm])

1" (3 cm) coarse sand

3" (8 cm) washed gravel

landscape cloth

*Figure 14. A standard, flexible path base on well-draining soil*

**2.** When figuring the amount of gravel for a path base prepared with a drainpipe (which fills a "V" shaped trough the length and half the width of the path, see Figure 21, page 57), multiply the length of the path times half the width, and multiply the result by the depth of the layer (in feet or meters). This will give you the material amounts you need in cubic feet or meters. Again, divide the number by 27 to determine how many cubic yards you need.

> **Example: Calculating amount of gravel needed for a base with a drainpipe.**
> Path length: 30 feet (9 m)
> Path width: 4 feet (1.2 m)
> Gravel depth: 3 inches or .25 feet (.07 m)
> 30 x 2 (half the width) x .25 = 15 cubic feet (or .42 m³)

## Alternative: Pouring a Concrete Base

A concrete base is more labor intensive, but it ensures an even, finished surface that won't settle or shift.

You'll need the following special tools and equipment.

- Bagged (dry) pre-mixed concrete or Portland cement (a bonding agent) plus sand and/or gravel for mixing your own concrete
- Tub or wheelbarrow and hoe to mix cement or a rented power cement mixer (An electric cement mixer is easiest for most work. Gas mixers are an option for large jobs and remote locations without power.)
- Mason's float (a small, flat tool much like a trowel) for smoothing wet concrete
- Hammer, nails, stakes, and framing lumber for making form boards
- Hose with an adjustable spray nozzle
- Plastic sheeting to protect the curing concrete from rain or other inclement weather while it sets

Dig out a bed approximately 8 inches (21 cm) deep, depending on the thickness of your paving material.

On each side of the bed, remove approximately 4 to 6 inches (10 to 15 cm) of additional dirt about 3 to 4 inches (8 to 10 cm) deep for setting the form boards. Tamp the base well. A hand tamping tool is usually best; powered tampers can drop the grade an inch (3 cm) or more. If the soil is firm, you'll be able to pour the concrete directly onto it (after making any necessary adjustments for a cross slope, if desired).

If the soil is unstable, you'll need to reinforce the base as follows:

**1.** To reinforce the base by adding strength to the concrete, use either wire mesh or rods of #4 steel rebar (both should be set up on rocks or brick chunks so the cement will flow around them). You can also mix fiberglass into the wet concrete to make it stronger.

**2.** On the sides, put in form boards to hold the concrete when it's poured. You can make these from pieces of scrap lumber held in place every 3 to 4 feet (1 to 1.2 m) by wooden stakes driven into the ground against the outside of the boards and nailed in place. Strips of 4-inch- (10-cm) wide particle board work well as form boards on curves. On flat slopes, you can pre-nail the stakes to the form boards. On rolling grades, it's easier to set the form boards in the bed, drive stakes in behind the boards, and nail the boards to the stakes (supporting the stake behind with a stone mason's hammer). These forms help establish a strong edge and can be checked with a level to monitor the grade of the concrete base. Once the concrete is set, the forms can be ripped out and discarded (or reused). You can also leave them in place and cover them with dirt.

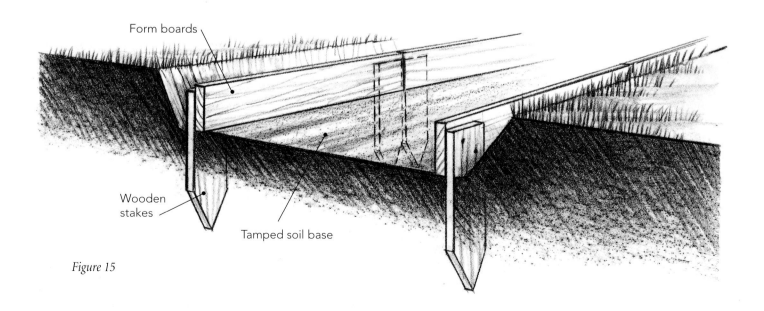

Form boards

Wooden stakes

Tamped soil base

*Figure 15*

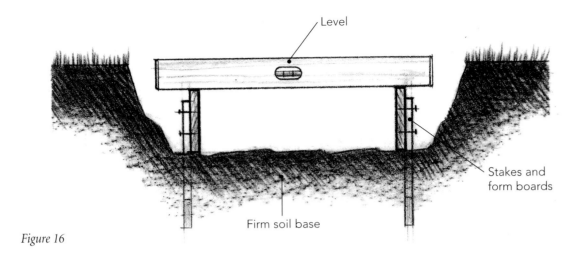

*Figure 16*

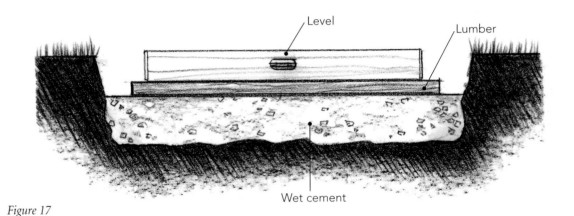

*Figure 17*

Figure 15 shows a path base prepared with form boards.

A good concrete mix for this base would be 1 part Portland cement, 2 parts clean river sand, and 3 parts gravel. You can either mix the cement with a hoe, rent a cement mixer, or call a company that delivers ready-mixed cement, depending on how ambitious you are and how much ground you have to cover. The surface of a concrete base need not be very smooth, but if you want your path to have a cross slope, the concrete base

should have one as well. Rest a level on the form boards, if you're using them (see Figure 16), and adjust their height as necessary to maintain the desired cross slope. If you're not using form boards, place the level on a piece of lumber laid flat across the wet cement (see Figure 17).

Allow the concrete to set overnight. On the concrete base, you can either dry-lay stones or bricks on a settling bed of sand or, for maximum stability, mortar

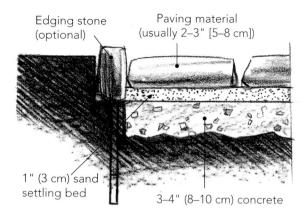

Edging stone (optional)

Paving material (usually 2–3" [5–8 cm])

1" (3 cm) sand settling bed

3–4" (8–10 cm) concrete

*Figure 18. Dry-laid stone on a concrete base*

*Figure 19. Drainpipe*

*Figure 20. Drainpipe and sock*

them in place. Figure 18 shows a cross section of dry-laid stone on a concrete base.

## Improving Drainage

Correcting drainage is a site-specific job. If your soil drains poorly but your path is sloped to drain or carry water, you might not have any problems. If your path slopes steeply, you may find it best to build in water break troughs at various intervals to help water drain during heavy rains. Following are some general guidelines for improving drainage. If you have specific concerns or live in an area where drainage is poor, you may want to consult other references, including books geared toward site grading and site engineering, and/or consult a landscape architect or a civil engineer.

## Adding a Drainpipe

If the soil test (outlined on page 20 of the Getting Started chapter) indicates poor drainage, you can compensate for it by adding a drainpipe when filling in your base materials.

Lay down just 1 inch (3 cm) of gravel, then place a perforated, 4-inch (10-cm) plastic drainpipe along the center of the base. The drainpipe should run the length of the path and continue away from the low point to a ditch or low spot where water naturally runs off. To prevent sediment from filling the pipe, you can wrap it with a landscape cloth, use a sock designed to cover the pipe (some pipes come with the sock already surrounding it), or cover the gravel base with a landscape cloth (see Figures 19, 20, and 21). After laying the drainpipe, fill the trench with 6 inches (15 cm) of gravel and 1 inch (3 cm) of sand, again leaving several inches for paving material. (In this

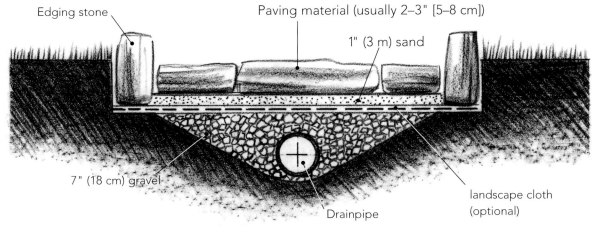

Edging stone

Paving material (usually 2–3" [5–8 cm])

1" (3 m) sand

7" (18 cm) gravel

Drainpipe

landscape cloth (optional)

*Figure 21. Standard, flexible path base with a drainpipe*

case, rather than making the finished surface just above the surrounding ground, it should be flush with the ground.)

Figure 21 shows a cross-section of a path base prepared with a drainpipe.

## Adding a Water Break Trough

If your path slopes steeply, you may want to add a water break trough to assist with drainage and reduce erosion of a gravel or natural material path. This trough is a two-sided ditch that runs across the path at intervals along a steep slope.

Dig a trench 5 inches (13 cm) deep by slightly more than 8 inches (21 cm) wide. Build the trough by nailing two 8-foot-long (2.5 m) pressure-treated 2x4-inch (5x10-cm) boards to an 8-foot-long (2.5 m) pressure-treated 2x8-inch (5x21-cm) board. Connect the 2x4-inch (5x10 cm) boards with two galvanized bolts that are approximately ⅜-inch (1 cm) in diameter and spaced at even intervals with nuts and washers on

each side of the boards. The trough should be set into the trench at a slope of at least two percent (it may slope more, depending on the downward angle of the trough across the path); see Figure 22.

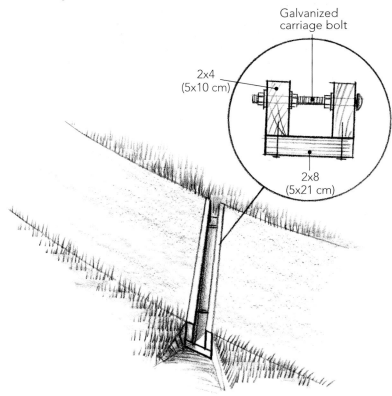

Galvanized carriage bolt

2x4 (5x10 cm)

2x8 (5x21 cm)

*Figure 22*

## Setting Edging

Edging helps contain your path, keeping soil, grass, and weeds from creeping in and loose paving material from spilling out. Though you may decide it's unnecessary for informal paths, edging enhances durability and adds detail and style.

Usually, it's easiest to dig a shelf in the base and set the edging during the excavation of your path base before you add paving material. However, if you plan to simply line the edges of your path with field stones set on top of the ground or accent it with a creeping peren-

nial, you can add the edging after you've completed the path surface.

Common edging materials include:

- Wood, such as 2x4- or 2x6-inch (5x10- or 5x15-cm) boards. (Most woods rot quickly in soil, so use pressure-treated wood.)
- Pre-formed plastic or metal edging, available at gardening and landscape centers. (Opt for ¼-inch [1-cm] commercial-grade metal edging, which is much more durable than the thinner, residential-

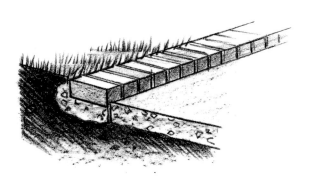

Mortared brick edging

Timber

Quarried stones

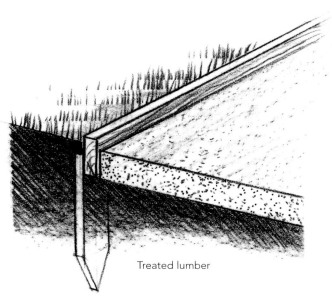

Treated lumber

*Figure 23*

grade edging. These forms of edging usually come with loops attached at the base through which you drive stakes to hold the edging in place.)

- Stone or brick that is identical or complementary to your paving material.
- Myriad other materials. Be creative; everything from ornamental tiles and concrete blocks to cockle shells can make appropriate edging in the right setting.

Figure 23 shows various edging materials and designs.

If you're edging with stone, brick, or another material in a lawn area, set the upper surfaces of the edging just at or not more than ½ inch (1.5 cm) above ground level so it won't be an obstacle to lawn mowers. If you're using a landscape cloth, set the edging on top of it to hold it in place (see Figure 24).

To use timber as edging, dig a shelf along your path that is deep enough to bury half the timber. Then drill ⅝-inch-diameter (1.6 cm) holes through each timber, spacing the holes 3 or 4 feet (1 or 1.2 m) apart. Position the drilled timbers on the gravel base (or on the landscape cloth that covers the gravel). Then, using a sledge hammer, drive 2-foot lengths (.6 m) of #5 rebar through each hole into the ground, sinking the lengths of rebar until they're flush with the tops of the timbers.

*Figure 24*

# CHAPTER SIX

# CREATING PATHS & WALKWAYS

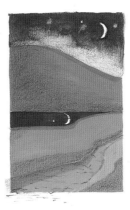

*It's little I care what path I take,*
*And where it leads it's little I care;*

. . .

*I wish I could walk for a day and a night,*
*And find me at dawn in a desolate place*
*With never the rut of a road in sight,*
*Nor the roof of a house, nor the eyes of a face.*

Edna St. Vincent Millay
"Departure"

# NATURAL MATERIAL PATHS

Natural materials—pine needles, bark, sawdust, leaves, the earth itself—make paths that look as inviting as weathered forest trails. They welcome travelers with soft, comfortable surfaces and pungent, earthy scents. These most informal of paths are also among the easiest to build. For details on using natural materials for path surfaces, see page 24.

## Base

If your soil drains well, you may be able to create a natural material path with no more preparation than clearing the surface of the soil and spreading on several inches of path material.

However, if you want to guard against a mud-filled path after a rain, prepare a deeper base. Dig a bed of 6 inches (15 cm) and cover the bottom with 3 inches (8 cm) of ½-inch to ¾-inch (1.5-cm to 2-cm) clean gravel or "crusher run." Rake the stone level and stomp back and forth on it to pack it, then finish your base with

*A natural path on a gently sloping site*

approximately 2 inches (5 cm) of bark mulch, which will provide a soft, springy foundation for the path's 1-inch (3 cm) surface layer.

If the drainage of your path area is especially poor, dig a base of approximately 10 inches (26 cm). Fill it with 1 inch (3 cm) of clean gravel, lay a 4-inch (10 cm) drainage pipe, then cover it with more gravel and a landscape cloth to serve as a sediment barrier. Finish the base with 2 inches (5 cm) of bark mulch—again, to provide a springy foundation underneath the path's top layer. (See page 56 for details on adding a drainage pipe to your path base.) Be aware that natural materials are fairly easy to kick through or lose to erosion, and nothing looks worse than a "bald spot" of landscape cloth peeking through a natural material path. If you use a landscape cloth, watch for this potential problem, and add more surface material when it occurs.

*This quiet mulch path curves toward a resting spot.*

*This pine-needle path is impossible to resist, as it curves out of sight in the distance.*

## Design

Designs for these unassuming paths should be as simple as their materials—the more natural-looking the better. Let them follow routes where people are already wearing a trail—to the boat dock, the neighbor's fence, or the climbing tree at the back of the yard.

## Adding the Top Layer

After laying the base, spread the surface material on top of the bark mulch. If you're creating a bark-mulch path, just add 1 to 2 inches (3-5 cm) of additional mulch as surface material (this means you will have a total of approximately 4 inches [10 cm] of bark mulch, including the base layer.) If you're adding another surface material such as pine straw or leaves,

# APPALACHIAN TRAIL

*Volunteer trail builders mount the Appalachian Trail terminus sign at Katahdin, Maine, 1937.*

*AT hikers number 3 to 4 million annually.*

FOLLOWING ON THE HEELS OF THE URBAN AND industrial boom that hit early 20th-century New England, a host of hikers and trail-building clubs sought to get away from it all—to escape urbanity for spiritual rejuvenation in the wilderness. Such was the inspiration behind the Appalachian Trail, or AT, one of the longest footpaths in the world built sheerly for personal recreation. Stretching 2,160 miles (3,456 m) from Georgia to Maine, it traverses 14 states by tracing the ridge lines of the oldest mountain chain in North America. The trail offers three to four million hikers a year a chance to reconnect with nature and to travel amid rich scenic beauty and peacefulness.

*Mt. Rogers National Recreation Area, Virginia*

**Summer, 1900** Emile Benton MacKaye clung to a treetop on the peak of Vermont's Stratton Mountain to gain a better view of the breathtaking mountains. He later wrote, "Would a footpath someday reach [far-southern peaks] from where I was then perched?"

**Oct. 1921** An article in the *Journal of the American Institute of Architects* gave reality to the dream of an Appalachian Trail. Its author, MacKaye, would play a pivotal role in making the dream a reality.

*Early trail builders*

**Oct. 7, 1923** A stretch of trail from Bear Mountain Bridge to the Ramapo River, completed by volunteers of the New York-New Jersey Trail Club, became the first official stretch of the Appalachian Trail. A dedicated corps of volunteers throughout the East performed much of the early construction and maintenance for the AT, a task they continue to perform as a labor of love today.

*Harper's Ferry, West Virginia*

**1933** The southern third of the AT plunged the trail into isolated backcountry, some of which had never been topographically mapped. This section was completed by U.S. Forest Service and local trail clubs.

**1934** 1,937 miles of the trail had been completed; only the state of Maine remained.

**1937** A six-man Civilian Conservation Corps crew completed the final link of the Appalachian Trail in the Maine woods on August 14.

**1948** Earl Shaffer of Pennsylvania performed the first "thru-hike" of the (at that time) 2,050-mile Appalachian Trail, making the journey in four months. Although many people considered him foolish for attempting the entire trek in one, uninterrupted trip, more than 300 hikers now thru-hike the AT every year.

**1958** The Appalachian Trail Conference moved the southern terminus of the trail 20 miles north to Springer Mountain, Georgia.

**1968** The U.S. Senate passed the National Trails System Act, which provided for a national system of trails, designating the Appalachian Trail as the first National Scenic Trail.

Maryland

Virginia

West Virginia

North Carolina

South Carolina

Georgia

*A short stretch of a pine-needle path leads to a tiny retreat amid concrete and a city street.*

add 4 to 6 inches (10 to 15 cm), since the material will compact.

## Maintenance

Materials such as pine needles and leaves will have to be replenished each year, and you may even have to add some as the year goes along. Other material, such as bark mulch, can simply be replenished as it decomposes.

## DRAINAGE FOR EARTH PATHS

Earth paths are familiar and welcoming, and they often "create themselves" as the product of human and animal traffic. They also share the disadvantages of natural landscape features, such as forming puddles after a rain and sinking below ground level under the weight of repeated footsteps. One way to improve drainage on an existing earth path is to add dirt to raise the grade. If the extra dirt doesn't improve the natural stormwater flow, you may want to bridge any troublesome swales in the path with logs, field stones, or simple wooden boardwalks.

*This natural path blends perfectly with the wooden landings and steps.*

# GRAVEL AND ORNAMENTAL STONE PATHS

*As you plant along the borders, remember that you may eventually share your walking space with blooming trees and flourishing plants (see above and right).*

Gravel, crushed stone, and decorative pebbles can be used to add texture, color, and comforting crunching sounds to paths in both formal and informal settings. These materials work especially well on curving paths and areas with slight slopes. For details on gravel and ornamental stone as path materials, see page 26.

## Base

The standard path base described in Chapter Five can be simplified for a gravel or ornamental stone path.

Simply excavate a bed 3 inches (8 cm) deep, and fill it with 2 inches (5 cm) of "crusher run" (also called "road bond"—an unscreened gravel with lots of granite dust and small particles that compact into a strong yet flexible base).

However, if the drainage of your path area is especially poor, dig a base of approximately 7 inches (18 cm). Fill it with 1 inch (3 cm) of clean gravel, lay a 4-inch (10-cm) drainage pipe, then cover it with more gravel and finish with a landscape cloth. (See page 56 for details on adding a drainage pipe to your path base.)

Add an edging material (see page 58) before filling in the top layer. Edging is essential to keep gravel or ornamental stone in place.

## Design

Gravel and loose rock can be used to create everything from straight, neat walks to formal pleasure gardens or narrow connector paths that wind through trees or behind tool sheds. Along with the path layout, the color and texture of the gravel or pebbles will affect the look you achieve. For example, as angular pieces of fine-textured crushed stone settle into a path, it will begin to look more natural and pleasantly timeworn. Rounded, decorative pebbles on a path lined with a

*From left to right: Fieldstone edging adds charm to this gravel path; "granite gravel," or decomposed granite, is a popular paving material in the Austin, Texas, area. At the Austin Area Garden Center, they've used pieces of limestone for edging; this gravel path provides a comfortable transition from a grassy area—and is welcoming to travelers of all kinds.*

# The Silk Road, Ancient Lifeline of Asia

LONG BEFORE ASPHALT, WHITE LINES, AND rubber tires came to define land travel and commerce, dusty trade routes were cut into the earth by the footfalls of millions of human travelers and pack animals. The Silk Road was the most magnificent of these routes, spanning more than 4,000 miles (6,400 km) of the desert and steppe country between China and the Mediterranean. Dedicated traders, explorers, and middlemen (who profited by transporting goods for producers and retailers) traveled this path—almost exclusively on foot—risking their lives to sandstorms and raiding parties. Some sought the fine silks and exotic spices at the road's eastern end. Others packed up wool,

gold, and silver from the West to sell in China. This awesome and legendary pathway served as one of the few links between Eastern and Western peoples, ideas, and products for nearly 4,000 years. Eventually it was disrupted by closed borders and civil wars and bypassed by new routes of sea travel, vanishing finally beneath the drifting sands.

***Circa 2000 B.C.*** Earliest descriptions of the Silk Road.

***Circa 115 B.C.*** First official records of the Silk Road as a trade route, developed primarily through Chinese efforts to connect their nation to the Mediterranean region.

***6th century A.D.*** An anonymous Christian writer penned common Western criticism of the Silk Road when he chastised "men who [could not] be put off from going to the ends

of the earth to fetch silk just for greed of money."

**1298 A.D.** Marco Polo brought the Silk Road to the world with the *Book of Marco Polo,* which described his famous 12-month trek across Asia with his uncle and father.

**13th century A.D.** Genghis Khan and his successor ushered in the Pax Mongolica, an era when most of Asia was united under the Mongols. The Silk Road was kept safe by Mongol soldiers, encouraging droves of European traders to brave the journey and spread the legend of the Road.

**1453** The city of Constantinople fell to the Turks, who sliced the Silk Road in two and hindered commercial travel.

**Late 1400s and early 1500s** The discovery of new sea routes made many land highways obsolete. Maritime travel allowed traders to avoid the Road's boundary disputes and profit-sharing with middlemen.

**Late 19th century** The ancient trade route was rediscovered and officially christened "die Seidenstrasse," the Silk Road, by German explorer Baron Ferdinand von Richthofen.

**20th century** Today, the Silk Road is best traveled in one's imagination. No longer existing in physical form, its route passes through closed borders and war zones. Cities that once lined the Road lie buried under sand dunes hundreds of feet high.

*Mortared brick provides formal edging for a path that leads to an ornate iron gate.*

boxwood hedge, on the other hand, will create a much more manicured look. Colors that blend well with other landscape features near the path and that complement the colors of surrounding flowers and plants will add to the serenity and natural quality of your path site. And though contrasting colors—say, cool-colored gravel against a rich green lawn—can create a striking appearance, bright white gravel or marble chips tend to be too stark a contrast in most settings.

## Adding the Top Layer

After compacting the base materials, you should be 1 inch (3 cm) below the surface of the surrounding ground. Add your top layer of gravel or ornamental stone, bringing it just to or slighty above grade level. Rake the path smooth, water it, then tamp it or go over it with a lawn roller.

## Maintenance

If you're after a neat, well-groomed look, rake the path regularly. On a sloping path, you'll need to rake the gravel upward, since gravity and rain will tend to work it downhill. Weeds hoe out easily in loose gravel, and your surface layer shouldn't need to be replenished for several years unless the path gets lots of heavy traffic.

# GRASS PATHS

*A plush grass path at a South Carolina residence*

A grass path is one of the easiest and least expensive types of path to build. Ribbons of natural green that run between beds of flowers, shrubs, hedges, and ornamental grasses and merge with surrounding lawn and countryside can be created in several ways, as described below. For details on grass as a path material, see page 28.

## You Will Need

In addition to the basic tools and equipment outlined in Chapter Four, you'll need the following.

*If you're creating a grass path by mowing an existing field or lawn:*
- Lawn mower or tractor-mounted mower
- Edger, used to cut sod back from flower beds or other edges

*If you're using sod to lay a grass path:*
- Hatchet for cutting sod
- Rototiller (optional; can be rented)
- High-phosphate or super-phosphate fertilizer
- Kneeling board
- Sod staples (These heavy, wire staples, available at garden supply centers or made out of coat hangers, keep newly laid sod in place on steep slopes or on drainage swales.)
- Hose with sprinkler

*If you're seeding a grass path on bare earth:*
- Rototiller (optional)
- High-phosphate or super-phosphate fertilizer
- Drop-seeder (This rolling seeder, available for rent from equipment supply centers, will distribute your seed better than a "broadcast" seeder that hangs around your neck.)
- Hose with sprinkler
- Hay or straw for mulch

## Base

To create a grass path, there's no need to lay the standard path base described in Chapter Five. For the first two approaches outlined below, simply shape a path out of existing grass or field. For the second two approaches, prepare the soil for either sod or seed by breaking up the top 1 inch (3 cm) or so for good root contact or a good seed bed.

It's best to set edging before you make the grass path, but you can install it afterwards, or cut a 2 to 3 inch (5–8 cm) ditch along the path edge and fill it with mulch once you've finished.

## Mowing a Grass Path out of a Field

Once you've decided how you want your path to flow (perhaps following a fence line or curving gracefully toward a gate) mark the centerline by wrapping marking tape around bunches of tall grass or wildflower stalks. You can let the width of the mower determine the path width—one pass wide for a tractor-mounted mower, two passes for a riding lawn mower. Set the blades on your mower to low and mow the course you've marked, then remove the grass clippings from the path. That's it! This easiest of paths is most appealing when it flows with the gentle roll of the land, and it's perfect for linking lawns with surrounding countryside. To keep it healthy and green, mow it once or twice a month. You can let the grass bordering the path grow as high as 3 feet or more (1 m or more), mowing it only seasonally or even yearly.

## Making a Grass Path in an Existing Lawn

Tired of that plain, boring lawn? Try converting it to a grass path that winds between beds of plants. Begin by marking the outline of the path. Then, use an edger or

*A mown grass path*

shovel to slice into the turf and define the borders of the path. Remove the sod from areas that are to be flower beds, using a foot adz, mattock, flat shovel, or, if the area is large, a rented sod cutter. (The sod can be transplanted to worn spots in the yard or used to re-shape plant beds.) Place edging along the path to add definition and to prevent grass from creeping into the surrounding flower beds. (For details on types of edging, see page 58.) The edging should be less than 1 inch (3 cm) above with the grade if you want to avoid hand trimming each time you mow. Finally, pre-pare the soil in the beds for planting and fill them with herbs or flowering plants. This is an easy path to create if your site is already full of beds that can sim-ply be re-shaped, extended, or joined to form grass walkways between them.

## Laying a Sod Path or Sowing a Grass Path

There are several reasons why you might choose to lay a sod path rather than sow grass seed. First, sod paths are ready to view and use soon after you've finished laying them; grass seeds need three or four weeks of undisturbed time and good weather to germinate and grow. Plus, seasonal sod can be laid anytime of year other than deep winter (and even winter may be fine for growth if you're in a southern climate). Seeds, on

*A perennial border was renovated to create this path.*

the other hand, do best when they're sown in fall or in early spring. (If they're sown in the summer, they'll require persistent watering.) Also, sod does well on sloping path sites, where seeds can wash away in a heavy rain, and certain hybrid grasses are available only as sod. Finally, while weeds will sprout along with grass seed, sod smothers potential weeds underneath it.

So why would anyone plant seed? Laying sod is more expensive, and it's much heavier work.

## Preparing the Soil

Regardless of whether you use sod or seed, begin by sending a soil sample from your path area to the local agricultural extension office or testing lab. The results of the soil test will tell you how to treat your soil to produce a healthy lawn. Next, after marking the borders of your path, clear the site completely, removing all rocks, roots, weeds, and unwanted grass. Cut out grass with a flat-nosed shovel or a foot adz (or a rented sod cutter if you're clearing a large area). If the soil is heavy, break it up with a hard rake or mattock or till it with a rototiller so that the roots of your new sod will be able to penetrate it.

The results of the soil sample test will tell you whether you need to spread lime (to raise your soil's pH level) and/or add a high-phosphate starter fertilizer that will promote root growth (0-20-0, for example). After treating the soil, break it up with a hard rake to a depth of a couple of inches (5 cm), then use the rake to smooth the surface.

*Dry-laid bluestone stepping stones lead to a grass path beyond.*

## Laying Sod

Timing is important when laying sod. Don't pick it up or have it delivered until you're ready to use it. In hot weather, it may begin to yellow and die if it isn't laid within about 12 hours of being harvested. In cooler weather, it will keep for several days.

If the soil is very dry, water the path area lightly (so the moisture in the sod rootlets isn't pulled into the soil), but not so much that your work space turns to mud. Then begin laying. Your sod will come in strips, usually 1½ to 2 feet wide (.5 to .6 m) and several feet long. Use a spade or a hatchet to cut it as necessary. Generally, it's best to begin at one end of your path and work toward the other. If your path is on a slope, laying the sod strips lengthwise across the slope will help prevent erosion. Where it's likely that the sod could wash downslope, you can use heavy wire sod staples to hold the uphill-side pieces in place (or all pieces on a diagonal slope). Remove the staples after the roots have taken hold (usually two weeks, or after the first mowing). Use a small piece of plywood as a kneeling board when laying the sod so that your knees aren't pressing directly into the sod you've just laid.

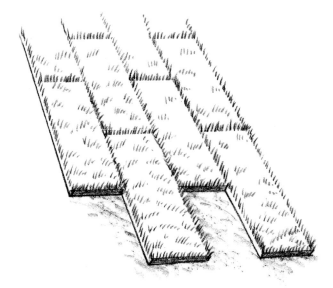

*Figure 1*

Be sure the individual pieces of sod are set tightly against each other to keep the edges from drying out. Also, to retain moisture, it's important that the joints between strips of sod alternate rather than meet from one row to the next. So, if your first row begins with a whole piece of sod, start your second row with a half piece, followed by a whole piece, and so on (see Figure 1).

When you've finished laying the path, use a lawn roller to press the grass roots into the soil and even out the bumps. This is very important; roots can dry out if air pockets are left between the sod and the earth. Sprinkle damp topsoil into any gaps between pieces of sod and the grass will quickly fill those areas in. Finally, set up a sprinkler to water the entire path deeply. In hot weather, water two or three times a week or more while the sod is getting established. At the same time, keep in mind that excessive watering can cause disease; your local agricultural extension office can provide guidance on how often to water in your area.

## Sowing Grass Seed

Check with a feed and seed store about the best turf grass seed to meet your needs; different seeds have different qualities.

Check the instructions that accompany your grass seed for recommended distribution (usually calculated in pounds according to square footage). A drop-seeder, which allows you to set a distribution rate, will help you sow seeds more evenly than you can by hand.

After spreading your seed, rake the entire path area lightly to mix the seed into the top ¼ inch (1 cm), of soil then roll it with a roller half-filled with water.

# The Lewis and Clark Expedition and the Lolo Trail

In 1804, President Thomas Jefferson ordered an expedition to explore the Louisiana Territory, the vast expanse of land the United States had purchased from France, and appointed Meriwether Lewis and William Clark as surveyors. The men spent two years traveling from St. Louis to the Pacific Ocean and back, meticulously recording in journals information about the flora, fauna, geography, and native peoples of the country's wild new terrain. The Lewis and Clark route was more than 8,000 miles long (12,800 km), and although much of it was traveled by boat, some sections followed ancient paths worn by Native Americans over generations of use. The Lolo Trail was one such route, used first by the Nez Perce people to cross the difficult terrain of the Bitterroot Mountains to reach buffalo hunting grounds on the plains of what is now Montana.

*May 14, 1804* Lewis and Clark set out from a winter camp at the mouth of the Missouri River in Illinois for the long trek to the Pacific.

*September 9, 1805* The expedition camped at the head of the Lolo Trail to gather supplies and rest before continuing their journey. They named their stopping point Travellers Rest.

*September 14 and 15, 1805* The expedition took a wrong turn and spent two days climbing the treacherous Wendover Ridge to remedy the mistake. While making the hard journey up the ridge, Clark wrote: "Here the road leaves the river to the left and ascends a mountain winding in every direc-tion to get up the Steep assents & to pass the emence quantity of falling timber…Several horses Sliped and roled down Steep hills which hurt them verry much."

*September 20 to 23, 1805* The expedition rested with the Nez Perce people at Weippe Prairie before continuing west. On the return trip in 1806, heavy snow forced the expedition to stay at Weippe Prairie again for several days.

*November 1805* The expedition reached the western edge of the continent. After failing to find a ship for return passage to St. Louis, the expedition retraced its overland route in the spring.

*June 27, 1806* Lewis and Clark smoked a pipe with their guides at a place marked with a rock cairn, halfway along the Lolo Trail in Idaho. Clark wrote, "…on this eminance the nativs have raised a conic mound of Stons of 6 or 8 feet high and erected a pine pole of 15 feet long… from this place we had an extencive view of these Stupendeous Mountains principally

*The Smoking Place*

Covered with Snow like that on which we Stood; we were entirely Serounded by those mountains from which to one unaquainted with them it would have Seemed impossible ever to have escaped, in short without the assistance of our guides, I doubt much whether we who had once passed them could find our way to Travellers rest… "

*September 23, 1806* Lewis and Clark ended their 8,000-mile journey at St. Louis, Missouri.

*1863* When a gold rush broke out in western Idaho, prospectors followed the Lolo Trail to reach the action.

*July 15, 1877* The Nez Perce people held council at Weippe Prairie and decided to flee the encroaching United States Army, using the Lolo Trail as their escape route.

*Glade Creek on the Lolo Trail*

Establishing good contact between the seeds and the soil will help ensure germination. Mulch the area lightly with marsh hay or straw to help retain moisture as the seeds germinate and the seedlings grow.

Don't mow your new grass path until the seedlings are 2 to 3 inches high (5 to 8 cm). When you do, be sure the soil is not too wet and your mower blades are sharp so you don't uproot the seedlings. After about five weeks, the root systems will be established and the path will be ready for foot traffic.

## Maintenance
Care for a grass path just as you would care for a lawn.

*This path begins at a bench (left), then winds uphill and joins a year-round garden (right).*

# STEPPING-STONE PATHS

*Don't create overly artistic patterns that require people to hop crossways from one stone to the next. Simple designs like this one attract many types of travelers.*

When imagining a quaint stepping-stone path ambling through a vegetable patch or winding into the woods, most people picture rough, randomly shaped natural stones. Rough stones do make a marvelous material for these casual walks, but you can also use decorative concrete pavers, more formal cut stones, or even wood rounds to create different versions of this easy-to-build path.

*An enchanting route through a bed of ivy*

## Base

In most cases, each stepping stone is set directly onto a patch of ground that has been excavated, sometimes with 1 or 2 inches (3 or 5 cm) of sand underneath to create a level base.

If you're concerned that harsh winters with deep freezes will heave your stepping-stone path, however, you can prepare the standard path base described in Chapter Five. Lay your stones on top of it, then fill in around them with the soil you removed to create the base.

## Design

Rigid design rules don't apply to stepping-stone paths, but there are a few general guidelines that will make your path more comfortable, functional, and pleasant to walk on.

- Because people have different strides at different speeds, stepping stones should be spaced with easy-to-cross gaps—1 to 4 inches (3 to 10 cm)—between them. If the path is to be primarily utilitarian, make the stones and gaps uniform. Stick with large, similar-size stones and space them close together. If the path is more ornamental, the design can be more creative, but don't stagger the path back and forth without a reason for doing so. A good rule of thumb to remember: If the path looks too difficult to walk on, the visual impression will be disturbing. Figure 2 (on page 83) shows a number of designs for stepping-stone paths.
- Typically, path builders lay stepping stones so that they cross the path route lengthwise rather than run parallel to it.

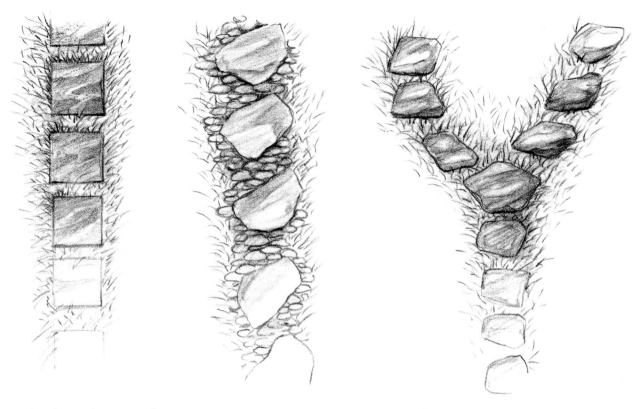

*Figure 2. Designs for stepping-stone paths*

- Stepping-stone paths are traveled by one person at a time, so your stones don't have to be huge—and might look out of scale if they are.
- Use larger, more identifiable "threshold" stones at the beginning of your path and at any transition point, such as where a separate path veers off.
- When choosing your stones, avoid concave shapes that will collect water. Also, stay away from smooth-surface stones (especially marble and slate) that will get slick in the rain. Pre-cast geometric pavers are better for straight, formal stepping-stone routes.
- Before you set your stones for good, lay them out and have a look, paying attention to how well the shapes and sizes work together. Ideally, you want them to form a harmonious pattern, looking a bit like drifted continents that were once connected.

## WOOD ROUNDS

Cross sections of trees, usually cut 8-to-10-inches thick (21-to-26 cm), make especially picturesque stepping-stone paths. You can cut the rounds yourself with a chain saw. Let them dry out, then soak them in a penetrating wood preservative before laying them. One warning: wood rounds aren't the best choice for wet climates or areas with poor drainage. In soggy soil, even treated wood rounds will eventually become covered with moss, making them extremely slippery.

# THE ANCIENT RIDGEWAY

THIS BRITISH NATIONAL TRAIL CROSSES 85 MILES (137 KM) OF southern England, tracing much of a pathway worn by travelers as early as 5,000 years ago. Following a ridge of the region's natural formation of chalk (remember the white cliffs of Dover?), the path offered ancient Romans, Saxons, and Vikings a safe, dry route to traverse forests and wetlands on the 240-mile (400 km) journey from present-day England's Norfolk coast to the Dorset coast. Earthen burial mounds, stone monuments, and hillside forts along the trail are evidence of centuries of use. More recently, in the 1700s and 1800s, the trail was used by drovers herding sheep and cattle across the English countryside, prompting farmers to build embankments and plant hedges along the trail to protect adjacent fields from livestock. During the Victorian Era, the Ridgeway was further enhanced by stands of beech trees to provide shelter for travelers. Though short sections today must contend with modern encroachments, including a major highway and a power plant, government and volunteer organizations work to preserve the Ridgeway and its surrounding land for future generations.

Barbury Castle

**Waylands Smithy** is an example of the Bronze-Age earthen mounds or barrows along the Ridgeway. It was named by the Saxons, who believed that a magical forge existed beneath the mound, ensuring that any horse left overnight would be shod by the god Wayland while the traveler slept. Archaeological evidence suggests that

Waylands Smithy

Rail bridge over the River Thames

these barrows were used as burial chambers. Long barrows such as Waylands Smithy date as far back as 5000 B.C.; similar rounded barrows date to 2000 B.C.

**Grim's Ditch**—which means "devil's ditch"—is the term Saxons used for the long earthen ditches, now nearly 2,000 years old, found along the Ridgeway. The ditches may have been constructed to confine livestock, for defensive purposes, or as property lines.

**Avery Stone Circle,** built at least 4,000 years ago along the

Beech trees lining the Ridgeway

Ridgeway near the Dorset coast, was likely a center for religious and social gatherings. This largest monument of its kind in Great Britain consists of huge stones, some weighing 50 tons, dragged into a circular pattern covering several acres.

**Barbury Castle,** constructed on a hill above the River Og during the Iron Age (1000 B.C. to 100 A.D.), is one of several forts built to protect travelers.

**Through the ages,** travelers have carved figures into hillsides along the Ridgeway, exposing a layer of white chalk that highlights each. The most famous of these is Uffington White Horse, shaped like a racing horse, created around 1000 B.C. Other hill figures were created as recently as the 1800s.

**1750** The Enclosure Acts led to the formal establishment of the current Ridgeway Trail. Planners selected one route from the several broad bands that followed the ridge line and defined it with earthen banks and hedge fences.

*Bluestone dry-laid in an irregular pattern*

## Laying Stepping Stones

Once you've developed the layout for your path and test-walked it to your satisfaction, set the stones one by one. Cut around the outline of the first stone with a garden trowel or a straight-nosed spade. Move the stone aside (leaving it in the same orientation it will lie in), and shave enough soil and/or grass from the space you outlined so that the stone will be flush with the ground when you set it in place. You may also want to excavate enough soil to allow for a 1- or 2-inch (3- or 5-cm) bed of sand, especially if the bottoms of your stones are uneven and won't balance firmly on flat earth. Set the stone and tamp it firmly in place with a rubber mallet. Repeat this process to set each stone in your path.

## Maintenance

Stepping-stone paths that run across a lawn may require regular trimming around the edges. The string blade of a "weed-eater" is a handy tool for this.

*Weathered wall stone laid in a setting of natural rock outcrops*

*Stepping stones work well in beds of gravel or ornamental stone.*

*Colored concrete pavers were used for this short crossing to a cut stone entranceway.*

*Stepping stones are often the perfect device for transitions from one area of the yard to another.*

## ADDING MOSS TO YOUR PATH

Moss matches the mood of stepping-stone paths especially well. Though you don't want it to make the surface of the path slick, it adds a wonderful, fairy-tale quality when used in the gaps between stones or as a ground cover around a shady path.

Propagating moss is a bit of a challenge, but you can transplant sections by hand from wherever you find them. (Nearby construction sites, drainage ditches, or any place where high-acid soil has been compacted and neglected are ideal; take no more than a palm-size cut out of a patch). Prepare the places where you want the moss to grow by pulling up all existing growth and watering until the ground is muddy. Gently water the moss patches, then press them onto the wet ground, water them again, and walk on them.

Moss has no roots or veins, so it must absorb its water from where it grows (meaning you'll need to water it lightly but frequently until it's established). Various mosses have evolved to survive in different environments. Sphagnum moss thrives in wet bogs, for example, while cushion moss lives on dry rocks. Be sure to match the moss you collect with the transplant environment. Wet, streamside mosses won't survive on a dry rock path, and vice versa.

# CUT STONE WALKWAYS

*Chinese pink slate is used for this formal walk. Note how the bordering shrubs are trimmed to mimic the paving pattern.*

Typically shaped in squares or rectangles, cut stone is a handsome and time-honored paving material. Cut stone is most often used to create paths and walkways that are formal and neatly kept, and it's best for straight paths or for paths with gentle arcs or curves. Types of cut stone vary by region; limestone, sandstone, bluestone, and granite are most common. For details on cut stone as a path material, see page 30.

## You Will Need

In addition to the basic tools and equipment outlined in Chapter Four, you'll need the following.

- Circular saw with a masonry blade, a sturdy piece of lumber to use as a cutting guide, and eye and ear protection if you need to cut your stone.
- Hose with adjustable spray nozzle

See page 53 for additional tools you'll need if you opt for a concrete base.

## Base

The standard path base described in Chapter Five works well for a dry-laid cut stone walkway. However, if your stone is thin, brittle, or especially small, you'll

*This handsome cut stone walk features bluestone.*

want more stability. You can either replace the gravel in the standard base with "crusher run" (see page 51), or pour the concrete base alternative (see page 53) and mortar your stones in place.

## Design

It's far easier to design a cut stone walkway by sketching possibilities rather than by moving around actual stones. Start by familiarizing yourself with the sizes and shapes of available stones. Then, using graph paper and pencil, make a scaled drawing of your path layout, copy it several times on a copy machine, and experiment with paving patterns. Graph paper you find in the school supplies section of the grocery or drug store is all you need. It commonly features a grid of squares measuring ¼ inch (1 cm) on each side. If you're playing with paving patterns for a small path area, let 1 inch (3 cm) on the graph paper equal 1 foot (31 cm); for areas that are larger, let ½ inch or ¼ inch (1.5 or 1 cm) equal 1 foot.

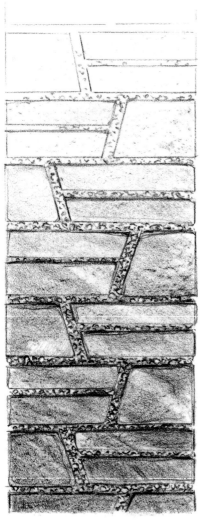

*Figure 3. Cut stone paving patterns*

Consider laying repeating patterns using stones of similar size, alternating square and rectangular stones, juxtaposing large and small stones, or setting stones on a diagonal. You can also combine cut stone with other materials, from bricks and tile to crushed gravel, or leave open spaces within the walkway design for planting a creeping thyme or another path herb.

If you're creating a random pattern with stones of different sizes, be sure to use one of your largest stones as a threshold to stabilize the beginning of the path. Smaller stones can dislodge if they're used along the edge of a cut stone path; save them for the interior, and use larger stones on the edges. Various cut stone paving patterns are shown in Figure 3. Once you've settled on your design, it will help you determine the number and dimensions of the stones you need to order.

## Cutting Stone

You may want to trim some of your cut stones to smooth their shapes or to adjust the shape to the edges of your design (especially if you are setting them on a diagonal). If you find you have a lot of cutting or need to cut curves into some of your stones, you may want to hire a masonry professional. If you're comfortable using a circular saw, you can make straight cuts yourself.

Here's how: Wearing eye and ear protection, use a circular saw equipped with a masonry blade to score the stone where you want to make the cut. As a cutting guide, use a sturdy piece of lumber. If you are only cutting off an inch or so (2.5 cm), go ahead and cut all the way through the stone. Otherwise, score it to a depth of about ½ inch (1.5 cm). Lay the stone on top of the wood, setting the scored line just above the edge of the board. Press or tap with a hammer on the center of the section to be removed, and it should snap off easily.

## Laying Cut Stone on a Dry Sand Base

If you're building a path on a slope, start at the low end of the slope and work uphill; stones settle naturally downhill. If the path leads from a house or another building, start at the structure and work toward the other end. If the path runs from one

# THE APPIAN WAY

*The centuries-old Appian Way was constructed of polygonial blocks of lava, smoothly and expertly fitted together, atop a foundation of mortared stone blocks. Engineers and builders—the latter group usually made up of Roman convicts—built drainage ditches and curbing along the road and elevated the center of the highway for drainage.*

THE APPIAN WAY, THE FIRST AND MOST FAMOUS of Rome's ancient roads, was crowned the "longarum regina varium," or Queen of Long Distance Roads, by Horace and Statius. Laid out in 312 B.C. by censor Appius Claudius Caecus, the Appian Way was the main highway from Rome to the seaports of southern Italy, Greece, and the Mediterranean for more than a thousand years. Not only did the glorious road provide unprecedented trading opportunities, it also united diverse and far-separated peoples into what was to become the formidable Roman Empire. And, like the cut stones and mortar that formed its foundation, the Via Appia supplied the backbone for the entire Roman road system. The infrastructure allowed people to travel thousands of miles in all directions, spreading Roman culture throughout the empire.

**298 B.C.** The majority of the Appian Way was covered in gravel during the first stage of construction.

structure to another, work from both ends toward the middle so that you're sure to place the best stones near the buildings.

Begin laying the stones on the sand, according to your paving pattern design. You can set them tightly against each other, but stones are rarely cut identically in the manufacturing process, and trying for neat, stone-by-stone fits may require much more additional cutting.

*Offsetting the seams between stones increases the strength of a walkway—and adds visual appeal.*

*The Appian Way first reached only 132 miles, from the Golden Milestone in the Roman Forum to Capua. The route eventually extended another 230 miles, traveling across the "ankle" of Italy to the Adriatic port of Brindisi, where traders could find exotic goods and spices from Africa, Egypt, and the Far East.*

**295 B.C.** Roman engineers began to use heavy, cut blocks of volcanic rock in road construction, eventually paving the Via Appia all the way to Brindisi.

**1st century A.D.** Early Christians used the Via Appia to run messages between communities hundreds or even thousands of miles apart. Persecuted members of this new religious sect were often forced to work at post-stations along the route.

**Middle Ages** The Appian Way fell into decline. Large portions became overgrown, and the celebrated causeway crossing the Pontine marshes deteriorated. Italians of the Late Middle Ages and Renaissance pilfered build-

ing materials from the Via Appia, using the stones from former monuments, post-stations, and the road itself to construct the walls of new churches and hospices.

**17th and 18th centuries** The Vatican took responsibility for restoring the Appian Way, draining the Pontine marshes and reopening a road across the land.

**20th century** The Appian Way continues to be a main thoroughfare in southern Italy. Though the road now bears the name Strada Statale (or State Road 7), and carries automobiles rather than animals, chariots, and foot travelers, many continue to refer to it as "the Appia."

*These cut stone steps blend with the adjoining path.*

If you want to avoid that, leave gaps of ¼ to ¾ inch (1 to 2 cm) between each stone. These spaces give you room for adjusting the stones and help with drainage.

After setting four or five stones, work them back and forth into the sand until they are situated where you want them, then tap each one several times with a rubber mallet to set it. Don't step on thin stones (stones less than 1 inch [3 cm] thick) until you've set them; they may snap if they're not evenly supported. Each time you set a series of stones into place, use a level to make sure the stones are even and the surface of your path is flat (or appropriately sloped, according to how you've graded your path). Placing your level on top of a 6-foot (1.8-m) 2x4-inch (5x10-cm) piece of lumber laid across several stones will ensure that crooked stones don't become inaccurate reference points for the entire path.

When your path is laid, spread sand over it and sweep the sand into the gaps between the stones. Spray water across the surface for several minutes, walking back and forth on the stones until the sand feels thoroughly wet and settled. You may need to add more sand to the gaps to bring them to about ¼ inch (1 cm) below the tops of the stones. The ¼ inch (1 cm) will keep the sand from spilling onto the path surface.

*Bluestone dry-laid on sand with an irregular border*

*Cut stone pavers with plantings in between*

*Above: Walkways and stair treads of pattern-cut bluestone; wall stone is used for the risers on the stairs. Below: Bluestone is used for a short stepping-stone path leading to a main walk of cut stone, all surrounded by blue chip gravel.*

## Laying Cut Stone on a Concrete Base

If you're mortaring your cut stone surface (rather than dry-laying it on sand) you won't be able to easily change your mind about stone placement, so be sure you're happy with your pattern before beginning. After allowing your concrete base to set overnight, use a trowel to spread a thin, ¾- to 1-inch (2-cm to 3-cm) layer of mortar on top of it and set your stones according to the pattern. Add more mortar to the gaps between the stones, using a trowel to drop it into the gaps and the edge of the trowel to smooth them. Neatness counts; wipe off any cement mixture that spills onto the stones with a damp sponge.

A standard mortar recipe is one part dry cement to three or four parts sand. You can tint the mortar you use to fill the gaps with coloring agents (sold where cement is sold) so that it blends well with the color of the stone.

## Maintenance

Dry-laid stone may need occasional reworking to keep the surface smooth. Tree roots may need to be cut out and the surrounding stones reset from time to time. If the sand in the gaps between stones washes out or settles in too deeply, you may need to add more. Finally, you'll want to weed the cracks between the stones as needed.

Mortared stone on a concrete base should require no more maintenance than occasional sweeping.

# NATURAL STONE PATHS

Randomly shaped stones of all kinds make charming, informal paving material for paths. Fieldstone, collected from fields or old dry-laid walls, often has an appealing rough or weathered look. Quarried stone, dynamited or pried from large veins in the earth, can have a jagged, stark, or clean appearance. Common types of quarried stone include sandstone, granite, and limestone. For details on natural stone as a path material, see page 32.

*Spicata grass makes a striking edging for natural stone paths.*

## You Will Need

In addition to the basic tools and equipment outlined in Chapter Four, you will need the following.

- Mason's chisel for breaking stone
- Hose with adjustable spray nozzle

## Base

The standard path base described in Chapter Five works well for a dry-laid stone walk. However, if you plan to use only small stones for your walk, you'll want more stability. You can either replace the gravel in the standard base with "crusher run" (see page 51) or pour the concrete base alternative (see page 53) and mortar your stones in place.

## Design

Because the shapes of natural stones are so variable, you won't be able to plot your path design at the kitchen table as you could for a cut stone walk. You'll have to design it on-site, and you'll have a number of interesting choices: you can use stones that have a similar size, outline the path with large stones and fill the center with smaller ones, develop a pattern of alternating shapes, or set the stones in a gravel path. Figure 4 suggests a number of paving patterns for stone walks.

## Laying Natural Stone on a Dry Sand Base

Begin by laying several stones along the outer edges of your path. Don't settle the stones permanently at this point—just set them on top of the sand. Next, fill in between the outer stones according to your design, shaping stones with a mason's chisel and/or hammer so that they fit together well. It's best to set the stones about ¾ inch (2 cm) apart, using larger stones on the edges and saving smaller ones for the center of the path.

## SHAPING STONE

Use a mason's chisel to score stones where you need to trim them and a heavy hammer to do the actual breaking, chipping, and shaping.

Once you have several feet of path laid out the way you want it, set the stones more firmly. First, settle them in place by hand, working them back and forth in the sand. (If you set the stones approximately ½ inch [1.5 cm] above the adjacent soil, the path will drain better.) Then, tap each stone with a rubber mal-

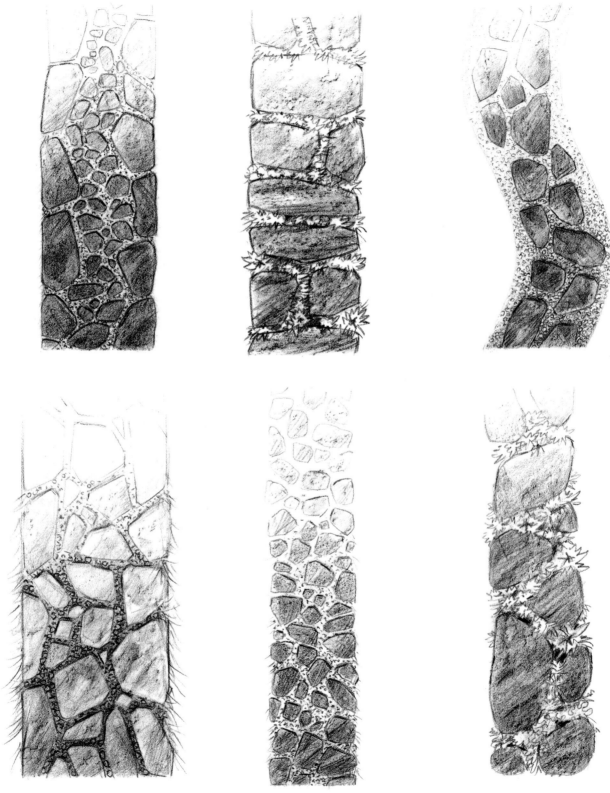

*Figure 4. A selection of paving patterns for natural stone paths*

# Santa Fe Trail

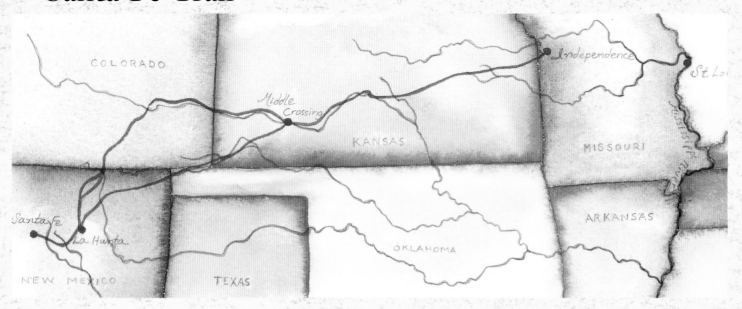

ONE OF THE BEST-KNOWN OF NORTH America's frontier trails, the 900-mile (1440-km) Santa Fe Trail carried thousands of people, cattle, and horses across prairies and over mountains from western Missouri to the Southwest, ending at Mexico's frontier outpost of Santa Fe. European traders blazed the Trail in the mid-1700s to reach isolated residents eager to trade for manufactured goods. After the Mexican-American War ended in 1848, pioneer families set out on the traders' route, joining together in "trains" of wagons loaded with necessities for a fresh start in a new land. Through its mountainous sections, the Santa Fe Trail followed footpaths established by the Pueblo and Anasazi people and later expanded by Navajo, Apache, and Comanche tribes. Eventually, the railroads replaced the much-storied wagon trains as the "iron horse" brought new crowds of settlers to the West. Some sections of track followed the old Trail, but most of the Santa Fe Trail returned quietly to prairie.

*In 1610,* Santa Fe, New Mexico, was established by the Spanish government as the northernmost outpost for Mexico. Far from centers of commerce, residents were eager to trade with anyone who would make the risky journey to their isolated location. Traders reached them both from Missouri and from Mexico.

*1792-1793* The Spanish government, briefly in possession of Louisiana, authorized Pedro Vial to survey the land from the Mississippi River to Santa Fe in

*While the trail provided a route to fortune and happiness for some of its travelers, others encountered hardship and grief. For Native Americans whose hunting grounds and settlements lay within route of the traffic, ways of life were harshly challenged and altered as the trail grew in popularity.*

*Wagon ruts, like these near Fort Larned, Kansas, are still visible along portions of the Santa Fe Trail, where in 1858 as many as 1,800 wagons passed through.*

*Pawnee Rock was one of the best-known landmarks along the Santa Fe Trail. Travelers often made camp at this halfway point, where they carved their names into the rock to immortalize their passage.*

*Natural stone paths often entice travelers to stay awhile.*

search of a new trade route. Vial's route would eventually become the Santa Fe Trail.

**1821** Mexico won independence from Spanish rule, and trade was officially opened between Santa Fe and the United States. William Becknell was the first to take advantage of the opportunity, leading a party from Missouri to Santa Fe. His successful trip is credited with opening the Trail to other trading ventures.

**1825** The United States Congress passed a bill to provide funds for a safe route between Missouri and Santa Fe.

**1846-1848** During the Mexican-American War, the Trail was an important route for the United States Army as it took control of Mexican territory.

**1849** The California Gold Rush increased traffic on the Trail.

**1869 to 1880** The railroad expanded across the Southwest, gradually making the Santa Fe Trail obsolete.

let several times to set it in place. If your stones have rough surfaces, a level won't always be accurate in making sure your path is flat or appropriately sloped; you'll learn to use your eye as well. If the surfaces of your stones are flat, however, use a level to check your path as you finish each section.

After laying the stone, fill the gaps with sand to within ½ inch (1.5 cm) of their tops and spray the path thoroughly with water to allow it to settle. The path will continue to settle as people begin to use it, so you may have to repeat the filling and watering process a time

or two. If you want to plant creeping plants or herbs or place bits of moss in the gaps between the stones, substitute topsoil for sand when filling the gaps.

## Laying Stone on a Concrete Base

If you're looking for maximum stability, the process for laying cut stone on a concrete base (page 96) can also be used for laying and mortaring a natural stone path.

## Maintenance

On an annual basis, at most, you may need to level some of your stones if you've laid them on a flexible base. You'll also need to weed the gaps and/or water any growth you're encouraging. Moss, especially, should be watered often, though lightly until it's established.

*Opposite page: Natural stones can create a more formal look. Above: A simple stone path leading through a garden gate*
*Below: Wide gaps between the stones and border plantings of purple thrift create a path that looks as if it might wind to a country cottage.*

# BRICK PATHS

Bricks are available in an array of colors and textures, making them a versatile material for everything from a front walkway laid in a formal design to a rustic path through a patch of wildflowers. For details on brick as a path material, see page 34.

## You Will Need

In addition to the basic tools and equipment outlined in Chapter Four, you will need the following.

- Brick sett (wide-bladed chisel) and hammer for cutting bricks, plus goggles (If you have a lot of cutting to do, you may want to rent a brick saw, which you should use only with gloves, goggles, and ear protection.)

- Kneeling pad (Insulation board or a piece of plywood will do.)

## Base

The standard path base described in Chapter Five works well for brick paths. However, you may want to consider two minor adjustments.

1. Your brick path will drain better if it is at least ½ inch (1.5 cm) above the surrounding grade (ground level), rather than flush with the grade. To achieve the slight elevation, increase the amount of crushed stone fill in the bottom of the base.

*This page: A brick path being mortared on a concrete base Opposite: The finished brick walkway*

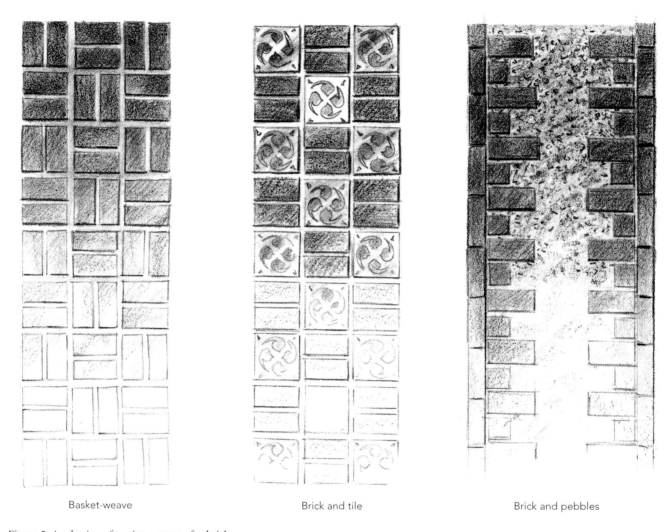

Basket-weave

Brick and tile

Brick and pebbles

*Figure 5. A selection of paving patterns for brick*

2. If you live in a region with hard-freezing winters and slow-draining soil, use a deeper base to avoid the danger of frost heaving, which can cause bricks to unsettle, by digging your path base several inches deeper and filling it with extra crushed stone. For added stability, use a concrete base (see Pouring a Concrete Base, page 53).

## Design

Patterns for laying bricks for a walk range from simple and symmetrical, such as running bond, to more elaborate and ornamental, such as herringbone and basket weave. You can lay bricks flat or stacked on edge, use them whole or in halves (halves are usually alternated with whole bricks in the design), or alternate bricks with sections of other materials, such as gravel or concrete. Figure 5 illustrates some popular brick-laying patterns.

How wide a gap you leave between your bricks will affect your design tone. Tightly laid bricks create formal-looking paths. Gaps of about ⅜ inch (1 cm)

Brick and pebbles        Herringbone        Diagonal running bond

between bricks create a more relaxed feel. What you fill those gaps with makes a difference, too. If you dry-lay your bricks and fill the gaps with sand, your path will look less formal than bricks joined by mortar. (If the mortar is a whitish contrast to the bricks, your path may look not only formal, but institutional. Think about softening the color of the mortar with a powdered tinting agent that can be mixed with the cement.) To add life and color to a dry-laid brick path, leave gaps by omitting entire bricks from your design,

then fill the gaps with topsoil and plant them with creeping herbs or perennials.

Finally, consider an edging material when developing your overall design. Edging is critical for brick paths laid on sand (see Edging, page 110) to keep the outermost bricks in place. The edging material can range from upturned bricks identical to your paving bricks, which looks somewhat formal, to weathered railroad ties, which are rough and informal.

*Both of these walks feature the popular "running bond" brick-laying pattern, but the end results are quite different.*

## Cutting Brick

To make a straight cut on a brick (such as cutting a brick in half), use a brick sett (a wide-bladed chisel) and a hammer. Place the blade of the sett along the cut line. With the hammer, tap it there and on the other three sides, then strike it more sharply (beveled edge away from you) along one of the scored lines. The brick should snap apart. If you plan to cut a lot of brick, you can make the job easier and faster by renting a brick saw, which is like a table saw with a water spray that keeps the blade cool. Always wear goggles and heavy gloves when cutting brick. Add ear protection if using a brick saw.

*These bricks were laid with tight gaps on a bed of sand, creating a neat, formal look.*

*Brick paired with bluestone*

### Edging

If you're laying a brick path on sand, use sturdy edging, such as treated 2x4 (5 cm x 10 cm) boards, to hold the paving bricks in place. Set the edging before laying the brick surface. Brick paths mortared on concrete don't require edging for stability, but most of them look better with an edge. For detailed information on edging types and procedures, refer to page 58.

### Laying Brick on Sand

One method of building a brick path is to lay the brick directly on the 1-inch (3-cm) layer of sand that tops the standard flexible path base. Wet the sand first with a hose, using a fine spray, then drag a screed over the sand (see page 40) to level the surface.

Begin laying bricks according to the pattern you've chosen. Work from a kneeling position, using a kneepad (such as a scrap piece of board or insulation) in the sand just ahead of where you're laying brick. As you lay each one, tap it with a rubber mallet to settle it. Use a level frequently to make sure the bricks are even and the surface of your path is flat (or appropriately sloped, according to how you've graded your path).

After laying several feet, spread sand over the completed section, sweep it into the gaps between the bricks, and water the section to settle it. You may need to repeat this process several times, until the sand fills the gaps almost to the tops of the bricks. (If the sand is too far below the surface of the bricks, the gaps may trap weed seeds and debris.)

# Capac Ñan ("Beautiful Road"): The Inca Trail

THOUSANDS OF YEARS AGO, traders carved the first long-distance routes through the mountainous terrain of present-day Peru, Ecuador, and Chile. But the Inca empire,

*View of the ruins at Sayacmarca*

which reigned in the 1400s, is credited with expanding the pathways into an extensive road system used for trade, warfare, and communication, with couriers traveling the paths to relay messages across the region. Two main routes formed the backbone of the Inca Trail: one traversed 3,000 miles of river gorges and Andes Mountains; a 2,000-mile sister route followed the Pacific coastline from modern-day Ecuador to Chile. They were connected by trails running east and west, designed with switchbacks and steps to ease the rapid changes in elevation for foot travelers and

their llama pack animals. The Inca empire maintained the great road through a program of mandatory labor. Ironically, the extensive road system that supported the Inca civilization also helped lead to its demise. A series of attacking armies, the last led by Spanish conquistador Francisco Pizarro, used the Inca Trail to invade and eventually topple the Inca's commercial and spiritual centers. Under Spanish rule, the Inca population plummeted, and the roads were left to fade beneath jungle overgrowth. Most sections that survived have since been superceded by modern highways and railroads. Over the last century, however, some portions of the old roads, such as the stretch from Cuzco to Machu Picchu, have been rediscovered and restored. Today, they are used by travelers eager to re-trace the ancient Inca routes.

**300 B.C.** Early inhabitants of present-day Peru, Ecuador, and Chile carved trade routes. Coastal and mountain communities previously separated by harsh terrain began swapping fish, salt, cotton, and tobacco for llamas, wool, and minerals.

**1000 A.D.** The Tiahuanaco people of the highlands around Lake Titicaca followed the trade paths to invade and defeat the coastal cultures.

**1300s** The Chimu empire emerged as the Tiahuanaco empire declined. Concentrated

*Chakicocha*

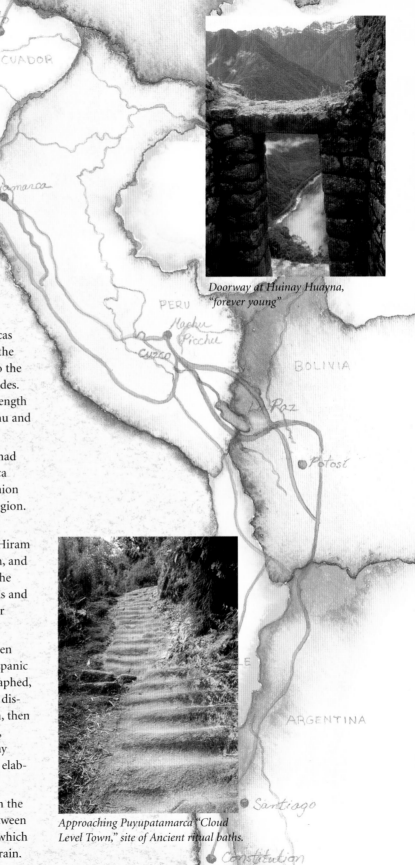

*Doorway at Huinay Huayna, "forever young"*

along the Pacific coast, the Chimu contributed significantly to the trail network by widening, marking, and maintaining the pathways. Many Chimu contributions, however, were destroyed or buried by later improvements.

**1400s** Under the Incas, who eventually defeated the Chimus, the trails were widened, curbstones and stone paving were used on heavily traveled routes, rocky cliffs were cut into stairways, desert routes were protected by adobe walls or marked with long poles, drainage systems were added to flood-prone sections, causeways were built across marshes, and suspension bridges were strung across ravines. Distance markers were used every few miles, and at mountain passes, stone cairns were built up by travelers who celebrated safe passage by adding their rocks.

**1532** Francisco Pizarro, after two previous contacts with the Incas, landed at the coastal city of Tumbez. The region's well-engineered road network enabled him to march his armies into the Inca's major cities and quickly conquer the empire.

**1532-1580** Following the Spanish conquest, many Incas used mountain sections of the road network to retreat into the highlands of the eastern Andes. They concentrated their strength in the cities of Machu Picchu and Vilcabamba.

**By the 1600s,** the Spanish had destroyed the last of the Inca strongholds to claim dominion over the South American region.

**19th and 20th centuries** Alexander von Humboldt, Hiram Bingham, Victor von Hagen, and others uncovered some of the ancient Inca cities and roads and amazed the world with their findings.

**1940-1941** The Wenner Gren Scientific Expedition to Hispanic America explored, photographed, and mapped the Inca ruins discovered by Hiram Bingham, then discovered additional ruins, including the town of Winay Wayna, characterized by its elaborately terraced landscape.

**1960s** Restoration began on the section of the Inca Trail between Cuzco and Machu Picchu, which tourists can now reach by train.

*Approaching Puyupatamarca "Cloud Level Town," site of Ancient ritual baths.*

## Mortaring Brick on Concrete

It's a good bit more work, but you'll get more stability and durability by mortaring on a concrete base. Because it will be a bigger job to change the path after you've finished mortaring, be extra-sure you're happy with your path layout and your surface design before beginning.

After allowing your 3-inch (8-cm) layer of concrete base to set (at least overnight), spread a ¾-inch (2-cm) layer of mortar mix on top of it and begin laying bricks according to your pattern. Use a trowel to drop mortar into the gaps between each brick, and smooth the gaps with the edge of the trowel. Neatness counts; wipe off any mortar that spills onto the bricks with a damp sponge or rag. As described in the sections on mortaring stone, use a level frequently to make sure the bricks are even and the surface of your path is flat or appropriately sloped.

A standard mortar recipe is one part cement to three or four parts sand. Consider tinting the mortar you use to fill the gaps with coloring agents (sold where

*Moss was used to fill the gaps in this brick and stone mosaic.*
*Opposite page: Bricks can be used to create both quaint and curving garden walks and gracefully arching entranceways.*

cement is sold) so that it blends well with the bricks and/or the path surroundings. Let the mortar set for at least a day before walking on the path.

## Maintenance

Dry-laid brick may need occasional reworking to keep the bricks level. Tree roots may need to be cut out and the surrounding bricks reset from time to time. If the sand in the gaps washes out or settles in too deep, you may need to add more. Finally, you'll want to weed the cracks between the bricks as needed.

Mortared brick on a concrete base should require no more maintenance than occasional sweeping.

# CONCRETE PATHS

Because you work with concrete in its soft (cement mix) form, you can use it to create almost any look you want. Concrete can be curved and formed into myriad shapes, used on steep slopes, poured into molds to create pavers, textured, colored, even decorated with anything from embedded crushed tile to shells. In just a day or so after pouring, it hardens into a durable walkway that will last for many years (depending on such variables as the weather, the firmness of the base, and the kind of traffic it has to bear). One caveat: once the concrete is set, there isn't much you can do to change the design without breaking the path to pieces and starting over. For details on concrete as a path material, see page 36.

## You Will Need

In addition to the basic tools and equipment outlined in Chapter Four, you'll need the following.

- Hammer, nails, stakes, and lumber for making form boards
- Expansion material for filling control joints in the path (This material, sold at concrete supply stores, is typically an asphalt-impregnated felt.)
- Bagged (dry) pre-mixed cement or Portland cement (a common bonding agent) and sand and/or gravel for mixing with Portland
- Tub or wheelbarrow and hoe to mix cement with water, or a rented power cement mixer (An electric cement mixer is best for most work. Gas mixers are an option for large jobs and remote locations that lack electricity.)

- Float: a flat, rectangular tool with a handle (similar to a finishing trowel) used for spreading and smoothing wet cement
- Edging tool (see Figure 8, page 118)
- Hose with adjustable spray nozzle
- Plastic sheeting to the cover the "curing" concrete during rain or other inclement weather

## Base

A concrete path can be poured directly into an excavated, compacted path bed approximately 4 inches (10 cm) deep. Follow the process outlined on pages 53-56 for preparing the soil and making form boards. Note that since you won't be laying a material on top of the concrete (your base and your path are one and the same), your form boards should come up to the "surface grade" (where you want your path surface). For added support, you may also want to nail in splice boards (small pieces of wood) where the ends of the form boards meet (to hold the form boards together). Be sure to nail the splice boards from the outside of the form boards—not from inside, where the cement will be poured—so they can be removed.

When warm concrete expands, internal pressure can cause cracking, buckling, or surface chipping. Expansion joints—gaps between sections of concrete filled with compressible material—help prevent this. Create them by placing expansion material anywhere your path abuts a structure such as a porch and every 12 to 20 feet (3.6 to 6 m) along the path, as well as any place where sharp turns or path intersections make cracking likely.

*Personalized concrete walk leading to a sundial*

*Concrete steps edged with brick lead to intersecting concrete and brick walks*

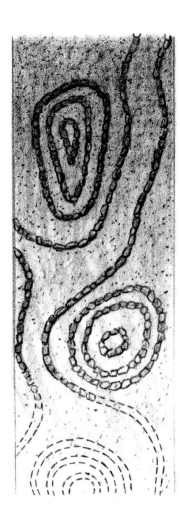

*Figure 6. Some designs for concrete walkways*

## Design

The most important thing to know about using concrete for your path is that you can't change the design once the concrete sets. Consider all design possibilities carefully before you begin. If your first image of a concrete path is a uniform, institutional walk beside a city street, you'll be delighted to know that many other options exist. Tinting agents (available in powder form at home and building supply centers, in colors ranging from brick-red to green or gold) can be added to the cement mix; so can materials that add texture, such as decorative gravel. You can enhance the surface of a concrete path by sprinkling it when wet with colored sand or by embedding it with materials ranging from colored rock or pieces of brick to crushed tile. Parts of the path can also be reserved (blocked off by boards) for other materials such as gravel, brick, or stone. See Figure 6 for a variety of concrete path designs.

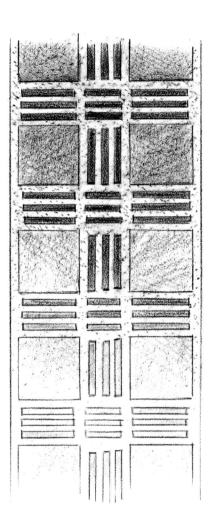

## Texturizing the Surface

To create an exposed aggregate look and feel for the surface of your path, mix decorative gravel with the wet cement, then wash away the finished surface of concrete with a stiff spray of water a day or two after pouring it. Timing the wash-off is critical; test boxes like the one described on page 123 should be used for experimenting first. If you spray the surface too early, too much concrete will wash out, leaving a pitted look. If you wait too long, the concrete will not wash out, leaving an unattractive surface of concrete covering most of the decorative gravel.

As another option, rock salt can be pressed into wet cement, then dissolved with the hose a couple of days after the concrete is set.

### Mixing the Concrete

A standard recipe for concrete mix for a path is one part cement, two and a half parts sand, and four parts gravel.

Mixing concrete is a bit tricky. If it's too wet, the ingredients can separate, which will cause cracking or uneven color. If the mix isn't wet enough, it may be too stiff to spread into the corners and air may be trapped along the edges. If that happens, you'll find gaps in the concrete when you remove the forms. To get the mix just right, pour a small amount in a test location before you pour your entire path. Pass your trowel across it; it should leave a smooth, glistening surface. If free water fills in where the trowel has passed, add more dry cement to your mix. If the surface is rough, add water, a small amount at a time.

## Pouring the Path

If you're covering a small area or plan to work in stages, you can mix your concrete with a hoe in a tub or a wheelbarrow, then shovel or pour it onto the path. For larger jobs, you may want to rent a commercial cement mixer, which does the hard work of mixing for you and allows you to mix bigger batches and pour it from the mixer into a wheelbarrow and then to your path. If your path site is accessible to a large vehicle, you can have the cement delivered by a cement truck. The driver can pour the cement directly from the truck onto your path by using a swinging chute. But be aware that the weight of the truck can leave deep ruts in a healthy lawn.

Once the cement is poured, push it into place with a shovel or a hard rake (not a leaf rake). Then, shimmy a screed back and forth as you pull it along the top of the form boards to distribute the concrete evenly (see Figure 7). It's best to have one person on each side of the screed for this job.

### IS IT MORTAR, CEMENT, OR CONCRETE?

Many people are confused by the terms cement, concrete, mortar, and all their cousins. Their meanings do overlap, so here's a beginning glossary: Portland cement is the limey powder you combine with water and aggregate—sand and/or gravel—to produce a mixture that hardens into concrete. Pre-mixed cement is Portland cement already mixed with sand and/or gravel; all you add is water. Mortar usually describes a cement mixture used as a bonding agent to lay bricks or stones. We'll leave stucco and the other cousins for another book.

Next, you need to smooth the surface with a float. You may want to use various floats, since different ones create different textures. Timing is important; you should work with the concrete as soon as possible after pouring.

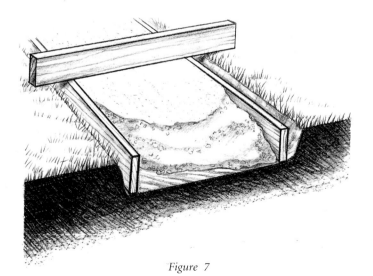

*Figure 7*

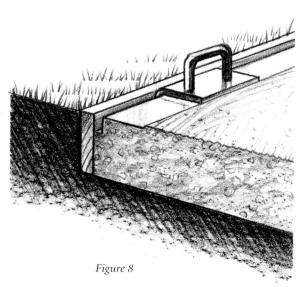

*Figure 8*

If you're not embedding the path with decorative materials, a common finish that provides a coarse texture is a "broom finish," created by working a stiff-bristled broom across slightly set concrete.

Finally, work around the edges with an edging tool (see Figure 8); shimmy it back and forth as you pull it along to create a smooth finish. Use this same tool to create 1-inch-deep (3-cm) impressions across the width of the path every 3 to 6 feet (1 to 2 m) or so (using a board as a guide). These "control joints" (like the lines you see in sidewalks) will help control cracking.

Cover the finished walk with plastic if it rains within one and a half days of pouring the cement. Also, mud can stain fresh concrete permanently; be sure to wash any off immediately. After about two days, you can pull out the form boards. The walk should be ready for your feet in three to four days.

A warning: Cement will harden on everything, from clothing to shovels, and its lime content is irritating to skin. Be sure to wear gloves, long sleeves, pants, and old or rubber boots when working with cement, and wash your tools as soon as you're finished. As you work, wash yourself often with a hose. Washing skin with vinegar helps balance cement's drying effect.

*Concrete pavers are used here with crushed limestone for steps in a path.*

*The concrete for this play-area pathway was stained and, while still in wet cement form, stamped with treasures including leaves, feathers, and shells.*

## Embedding Materials

Adding designs of embedded materials, from tiles to glass to shards of pottery, is a creative way to personalize a concrete path (see Figure 9). You'll need to work pretty fast; after about an hour (less if the weather is hot and dry) the concrete will become too hard for you to embed anything.

Have the materials you plan to add within reach, and mix and pour only enough cement to cover a few feet of the walk at a time. If you're embedding an elaborate design of many small pieces you may want to add a retardant, which you can buy at the hardware store, to slow hardening. Wear rubber gloves while pressing design elements into the surface. You'll probably also want to lay a sturdy board over the form boards on the edges of your path so that you can kneel on it while you work.

After you finish a section, lay a thin board or piece of plywood over the embedded materials and use it to gently tamp them level with the surface of the concrete. Once the concrete has hardened (probably the following day), you can sweep the surface clean with a stiff broom.

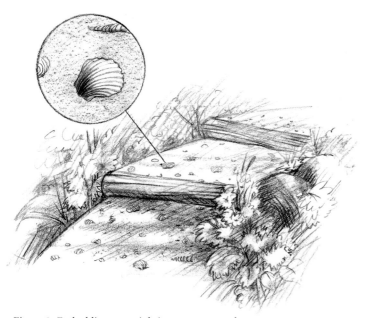

*Figure 9. Embedding materials in a concrete path*

# BLUE RIDGE PARKWAY

*Planners of the Blue Ridge Parkway envisioned a leisurely touring route that would provide spectacular views to a new motoring public.*

*Parkway architects used rock and other natural materials found in the region in the construction of the road's many tunnels and bridges.*

A CENTURIES-OLD MOUNTAIN TRAIL first blazed by herds of sure-footed buffalo now welcomes millions of human travelers each year, most of them rolling on two or four wheels. Winding 469 miles (750 km) along the crest of the Blue Ridge linking Virginia, North Carolina, and Tennessee, the Blue Ridge Parkway remains one of the most distinctive "pathways" in the world. Where else does a paved road cling to the very backbone of a mountain ridge for such a remarkable distance, offering spectacular panoramic views once exclusive to hawks and mountaineers? Throughout the decades-long construction process, Parkway planners maintained a commitment to environmental preservation, honoring the original impetus to make available the views and natural wonders of the region.

**Centuries before Europeans** arrived in North America, Native Americans traveled pathways along the Blue Ridge Mountains, using the routes to meet at tribal ceremonies as well as to raid other tribes.

*Marking a tree to be saved along old trail routes that would become the Blue Ridge Parkway, September 1936.*

**1700s** Moravian settlers trudged parts of the same trails as they carved out new homesteads in the rugged wilderness.

**1800s** Daniel Boone and Davy Crockett used the Blue Ridge routes on their hunting expeditions, probably tracking game and laying their snares not far from where the Parkway lies today.

**Late 1700s and mid-1800s** Soldiers of the Revolutionary and Civil Wars employed the paths as thoroughfares to battle.

**1909** The Blue Ridge Parkway was first conceived of and begun as "The Crest of the Blue Ridge Highway," a private toll road intended to showcase the natural beauty of the mountains.

**World War I** put a halt to construction until 1935, when it resumed as a Public Works Administration project of the Great Depression.

**World War II** officers found easy passage to mountainous terrain on the earliest stretches of the Parkway. They used these areas to train American soldiers before they left for European fronts.

**1985** With construction of the Linn Cove Viaduct in North Carolina, the Blue Ridge Parkway celebrated its final completion and the 50th anniversary of its commencement. After decades of administrative turmoil and funding dilemmas, the dream of a road that would follow the spine of the Blue Ridge was finally fulfilled.

*Many original historic sites, such as Polly Woods Ordinary, a rustic bed and breakfast built around 1840, have been preserved along the Parkway route and are now open to visitors.*

*Embedded concrete walk*

# PLANNING AHEAD

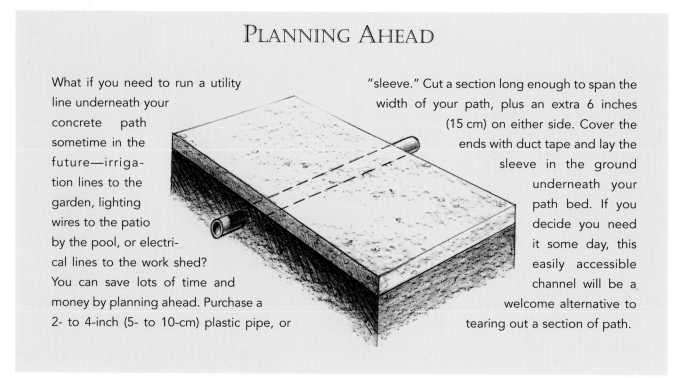

What if you need to run a utility line underneath your concrete path sometime in the future—irrigation lines to the garden, lighting wires to the patio by the pool, or electrical lines to the work shed? You can save lots of time and money by planning ahead. Purchase a 2- to 4-inch (5- to 10-cm) plastic pipe, or "sleeve." Cut a section long enough to span the width of your path, plus an extra 6 inches (15 cm) on either side. Cover the ends with duct tape and lay the sleeve in the ground underneath your path bed. If you decide you need it some day, this easily accessible channel will be a welcome alternative to tearing out a section of path.

*Colored concrete was used to create walkways through the Rainbow Garden at University of Michigan's 4-H Children's Garden.*

*A concrete "yellow brick" road*

## BUILDING A TEST BOX

When embedding materials, it's important not to overwork the hardening cement. Too much agitation causes a physical separation of the hardening agent and the aggregate. The overworked surface will start to look watery, which means that it may be weak and vulnerable to chipping (especially in freezing temperatures).

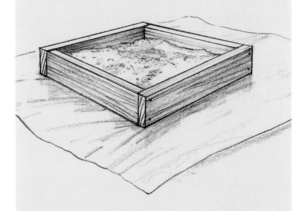

It's a simple matter to create a sample slab for practicing your embedding technique before trying it out on the actual path. Nail together four boards (each approximately 1 foot [.3m] long) to create a frame. Place it on a piece of plywood, plastic sheeting, or a large trash bag on a flat piece of ground or driveway. Pour in a small batch of cement, which you can mix in a five-gallon plastic bucket or a wheelbarrow, and experiment away.

## Another Option: Concrete Pavers

Concrete pavers have gained popularity as a surface material for paths. You can make your own using commercially available forms or you can purchase pre-cast pavers. Both forms and pavers are widely available at home and building supply centers. Pre-cast pavers are approximately 2½ to 3½ inches thick (6.5 to 9 cm) and come in various sizes and shapes, ranging from rounds and hexagons to brick-patterned squares or interlocking designs. Color choices are numerous too, from tan and black to weathered red, gray, and white (see page 36).

Pre-cast concrete pavers can be dry-laid in sand over a standard path base. They can also be laid on cement and mortared like cut stone. If you want to soften the uniform look of a path of concrete pavers laid on a sand base, leave out a paver here and there, fill the spaces with topsoil, and plant them with a perennial such as creeping thyme.

## Maintenance

Concrete paths are the most labor intensive to build, but the easiest to maintain. Occasional sweeping is usually all that's required.

*Opposite and above: Pre-cast concrete was used to create these pavers of simulated keystone.*

*Left. Moss-covered concrete meets broken tile mortared in place*

# GALLERY OF PATHS & WALKWAYS

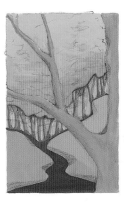

*I shall be telling this with a sigh*
*Somewhere ages and ages hence:*
*Two roads diverged in a wood, and I—*
*I took the one less traveled by,*
*And that has made all the difference.*

~Robert Frost
"The Road Not Taken"

The enduring charm of paths and walkways is that they remind us how we can elevate the useful to the realm of the artful. Some paths, of course, truly are works of art, designed for the sole purpose of providing an aesthetic experience. But most grow out of a need to get from here to there, and then, thanks to the pathmaker's vision, become oh-so-much more than a worn set of tracks.

This chapter is an inspirational, visual tour of some of the design techniques that can be applied—on any scale—to creating a path that is a work of art. It celebrates the act of transforming any journey—grand or small, leisurely or practical—into a joyous occasion.

*Travelers can't help but follow a path that curves out of sight in the distance, like this one at England's Wisley Botanical Gardens.*

*This path follows the logic—and layout—of nature.*

*The most inviting of paths, like this one at Ohme Gardens in Wenatchee, Washington, merge naturally with their surroundings.*

*The Bloedel Reserve, Bainbridge Island, Washington*

## Blending Form and Function

Paths can help solve practical problems through their design.

- If there's a direction in which you want foot traffic to flow (up the front walk rather than to the side door, for example), an enticing walk that pulls guests along can be just the inviting nudge they need.
- Paths are often the answer to organizational quandaries. They're pleasing ways to add structure to a place, whether they're helping to separate a patch of herbs from the rest of the garden or to mark a transition from the play area to the patio.
- Much more appealing than worn grass, paths provide comfortable access for people and equipment.

*Edinburgh Botanical Gardens, Scotland*

And if well-planned, they can reduce lawn and garden maintenance (less weeding and mowing) and help with other practical concerns such as controlling surface drainage and eliminating muddy areas.

*This page and facing page: Resting spots and sights along the way make a path irresistable.*

## Creating Patterns

The eye craves patterns. When one appears in the form of a path, the feet can't help but follow.

- The earliest paths made a formidable wilderness seem navigable, even inviting. Through the skill of their designers, paths can make sense of spaces, orient the walker, and show the best route to follow.

- As a path leads travelers along a logical route—through gates, around corners, toward benches, or under canopies of trees—it orchestrates their movement and shapes their experience.

*This simple gravel path winds beside a child's play area—complete with Rodin sculpture.*

*A formal, cut stone and brick walk with an Islamic fountain as the focal point.*

# LABYRINTHS

THE INTRICATE, INTERCONNECTED PATTERNS of labyrinths have been used for thousands of years to thwart invading enemies, ease passage to the afterlife, and deepen inner spiritual journeys. King Minos of Crete is credited by many scholars with constructing one of the first large-scale labyrinths as an entranceway to his palace at Knossos in 2000 B.C. There, legend has it, the mythic Theseus slew the Minotaur and saved himself by following a trail of string back out of the labyrinth. But not all early labyrinths were meant to entrap or confuse. Many served as meditative walking spaces to focus the mind and encourage spiritual reflection on one's own life. Labyrinths can be multicursal (with dead ends and a number of routes to the center, such as the Cretan labyrinth at Knossos) or unicursal (with no dead ends or illusions, offering a single route in and out). But all share three features: a mouth or entrance; a center or final destination; and a path or various pathways used to travel from the mouth to the center. Labyrinths can be constructed of nearly any material—simple stones placed along a route on the ground, hedges grown to great heights, bricks built into sturdy walls.

*A 17th-century Italian labyrinth*

**4500 B.C.** Some of the earliest known labyrinths were developed in northern Europe. Archaeologists have found the carvings of long barrows and megaliths from ancient camps in present-day Great Britain and elsewhere. Some spiral labyrinthine patterns are thought to represent the journey from birth to death, the pathway from this world to the next.

**3500 B.C.** The first tactical labyrinths appeared in Egyptian forts of the First and Second Dynasties. The structures included systems of walls with staggered openings that forced attackers to navigate long, crooked paths. This left them vulnerable to defensive actions from the walls and steps of the fort.

**3400 B.C.** One of the earliest Egyptian tombs, that of King Perabsen of the Second Dynasty, was modeled after a labyrinth. Later Egyptian tombs were constructed according to more complex labyrinthine designs.

**2000 B.C.** The first Cretan palaces were built, including the palace of King Minos, which was said to have a labyrinth at the center. Scholars continue to debate whether this famous labyrinth actually existed.

**1100 A.D.** Builders of Gothic cathedrals in Europe began installing tile or stone labyrinths in floors in the 12th century to be used for meditation and prayer. The labyrinth at Chartres, the most famous of this era, is 42 feet (13 m) in diameter. Worshippers who could not make a pilgrimage of great length or distance instead spent hours walking or crawling along the paths of the labyrinth.

**By the end of the 16th century,** elaborate garden designs were all the rage, and tall hedge mazes were a fashionable garden accessory. Hampton Court Palace near London boasts Britain's best known hedge maze, developed in this period. The Villa d'Este garden at Tivoli, built in 1549 and including at least four hedge mazes, was said to be the finest Renaissance garden in Europe.

**Late 20th century.** A copy of the Chartres labyrinth was transferred to canvas and circulated among modern churches, sparking a resurgence in labyrinths as pathways to spiritual growth.

*This wool tapestry labyrinth at Grace Cathedral in San Francisco, California, is based on the labyrinth in France's Chartres Cathedral.*

*Paths in the formal gardens at Biltmore Estate, Asheville, North Carolina, were designed by Frederick Law Olmsted, considered the father of American landscape architecture.*

## Setting a Tone

Paths, by combining purpose with setting, can play a central role in creating mood, whether you want a contemplative environment for meditative strolls or an adventurous route to a child's tree house.

- The character of a path, developed through layout, materials, paving pattern, edging, and ambiance, can suggest whether it's an ornamental pleasure path, a utilitarian walk, or a combination of the two.

*Above and facing page: The changes of the season will affect the look of your path.*

- With elements such as curves bending around corners, focal points in the distance, welcoming stopping points, and enchanting views along the way, paths can take travelers on journeys filled with expectation, wonder, exhilaration, and connection.

*The landscaping adds comfortable appeal to this otherwise formal path design.*

- By placing significant symbols along the way—from statuary to special plantings—some path makers transform their walks into personal pilgrimages filled with meaning, metaphor, and memories.

*A moss bridge*

*Above: Arbors, gates, trellises, and other structures can mark transition points in paths. Below: A brilliant display at Great Dixter, in southern England.*

*Above: A path that blends materials and shapes.*
*Below: Personalized stepping-stone pavers through a watery route.*

*Favorite paths often have a settled, always-been-there look.*

## Establishing a Sense of Place

Paths that look as if they belong where they are—as if, perhaps, they sprang up naturally—help create an environment of harmony and peace.

- Use paving and edging materials that are compatible in texture, shade, and scale with their surroundings. And don't introduce and combine too many materials or the path may seem more like a course of putt-putt golf than a pleasing part of the landscape.

*Clockwise from above: California orchard path; a distinctive pathway entrance; a stone path set into a front lawn.*

- Use existing features (both natural and made) as design elements. Consider how surroundings—rock outcrops, flowering shrubs, bird baths, fences, bridges, or fish ponds—might enhance the look and feel of your path.
- Employ the senses in establishing a sense of place. Traditional Japanese garden designers consider the way a path engages not only our visual sense, but also our sense of hearing (trickling water, the sound of the paving material underfoot, resident birds), smell (honeysuckle blooming at a curve in a path), touch (how it feels physically to your feet), and even taste (maybe the "flavor" of the path is dry or spicy, for example).

# ACKNOWLEDGMENTS & PHOTO CREDITS

*A number of special people deserve heartfelt thanks for collaborating on the creation of this book.*

*Dana Irwin and Katherine Duncan set it on its original path.*

*Randy Burroughs taught, wrote, built, sketched, loaned valuable resources,*
*and served as a wise guide, combining technical knowledge with a passion for making paths.*

*Heather Smith and Catharine Sutherland were partners in countless ways every step of the way;*
*their writing appears in the sidebars on historic paths (Heather Smith, pages 79, 84,*
*100-101, 110-111, and Catharine Sutherland, pages 64-65, 70-71, 92-93, 120-121, 136).*

*Celia Naranjo, puzzle master and artist both, gave the book not only form, but also beauty.*

*And Alan Anderson's contributions far surpassed those of a copy editor—he truly helped put ideas into words.*

**And thanks to the following people and firms from around the world who contributed photographs.**

### PHOTOGRAPHS SUBMITTED BY LANDSCAPE ARCHITECTS, PATH BUILDERS, PATH OWNERS, AND PHOTOGRAPHERS

Pages 103 (bottom), 112, 133, 134, 135, 139 (bottom right), 142 (bottom left): James M. Chadwick, Los Gatos, CA; James M. Chadwick, architect; Melgar Photographers, Santa Clara, CA, photographer

Pages 20 and 139 (top): John Cram, Asheville, NC; Doan Ogden, landscape design; "Saint Fiacre" statue on page 141 by Becky Gray

Page 141 (bottom left): City of Austin, TX; Natural Science Center staff, architects; Carol M. Foy, photographer

Page 119 (bottom): City of Austin, TX; Carol M. Foy, architect/photographer

Page 71 (top left): City of Austin, TX; architecture by City of Austin staff; Carol M. Foy, photographer

Page 125 (top): Michael/Todd, Inc., Naples, FL; Jeff Petry, ASLA, architect; William C. Minarich, photographer

Pages 119 (top), 124, 125 (top): Michael/Todd, Inc., Naples, FL; Jeff Petry, ASLA, architect/photographer

Pages 109 (top) and 132 (bottom): Dana Schock and Associates, Sudbury, MA; Dana Schock, ASLA, architect/photographer

Pages 31, 89, 96 (bottom), 108 (top): Hord Coplan Macht, LLC, Baltimore, MD; Carol Macht,

ASLA, architect; Bob Creamer, photographer

Pages 35, 76, 77, 85, 86 (left), 96 (middle), 108 (bottom): JOS Landscape Architect, Newtown, PA; Jayne O'Neal Spector, architect/photographer

Page 17: Ehrich & Ehrich Landscape Architects, Cranbury, NJ; Dennis Muhr, architect/photographer

Page 109 (bottom): Ehrich & Ehrich Landscape Architects, Cranbury, NJ; Dennis Muhr and Gary Hansen, architects; Dennis Muhr, photographer

Page 95: Simmons & Associates, Inc., Indianapolis, IN; J. Craig Hitner, architect; photography by Chilluffo Photography

Pages 16, 88, and 96 (top): Magrane Associates Landscape Design, San Francisco, CA; Penney Magrane, architect; Mark McLane, photographer

Page 87 (top): Barba & Groh Landscaping, Inc., San Juan, Puerto Rico; Gustavo Barba, architect; photography by Gustavo Barba and A. Thomas Groh

Pages 38, 63, 67, 73, 94, 101, 113, 115 (bottom), 142 (upper right), and cover shot: J. Dabney Peeples Design Associates, Inc., Easley, SC.; Graham A. Kimak, photographer

Page 66: Graham A. Kimak, Greenville, SC, landscape designer/photographer

Page 87 (bottom left): J. Dabney Peeples Design Associates, Inc., Easley, SC; Mark Maresca,

architect, Graham A. Kimak, photographer

Page 105: J. Dabney Peeples Design Associates, Inc., Easley, SC; Jack Thacker/Traditional Concepts, Inc., Greenville, SC, residential designer; Tony Pridgeon, Pridgeon Masonry, Spartanburg, SC, brick mason; Graham A. Kimak, photographer

Page 142 (upper left): Lutsko Associates, San Francisco, CA; Ron Lutsko, architect; Judy Adler, photographer

Pages 7, 68, 126, 137: Biltmore Estate, Asheville, North Carolina

Page 140 (upper right): Alpha Visions, Houston, TX (713-532-2345; www.alphavisions.com); Lynne A. Wiese, photographer

Pages 37, 115 (top), 122, 123: Michigan 4-H Children's Garden, Michigan State University; East Lansing, MI; photography by Norman Lownds, assistant professor and curator

Pages 22, 44, 129, 130: Ohme Gardens, Wenatchee, WA; Michael K. Short, administrator

Page 64: Alfred B. Maclay Gardens, Tallahassee, FL.

Pages 5, 131 (left), 138, 139 (bottom left): The Bloedel Reserve, Bainbridge Island, WA; Richard A. Brown, executive director and photographer

Pages 62, 75, 128,131 (right), 140 (bottom): Randy Burroughs, photographer

Page 60: Katherine Duncan, photographer

Pages 2 and 3: Dana Irwin, photographer

Pages 120-121 (color photos on each page): Max Keller, photographer

### SPECIAL PHOTOGRAPHY

Pages 8, 14, 84: National Trails Office, Countryside Commission, Department of Leisure and Arts, Holton, Oxford, United Kingdom; special thanks to Jos Joslin, National Trails officer, for photography and information

Pages 10, 12 (bottom): South Somerset District Council, Somerset, United Kingdom

Page 11 (top right and bottom): Thomas Rochford; Thomas Rochford, photographer

Page 11 (top left): Tourist Office of Spain, Miami, FL, office

Pages 12 (top left and right), 13, 136 (top): Christopher Thacker

Pages 64 and 65: Appalachian Trail Conference, Asheville, NC, office; special thanks to Valerie Shrader for her assistance

Page 70: India Tourist Office, New York office

Page 71: Michael Powers

Pages 79: Lewis and Clark Trail Heritage Foundation, Inc., Great Falls, MT; photography by Steve Lee; special thanks to Ludd A. Trozpek, volunteer curator

Pages 92 and 93: Italian Government Tourist Board, New York office

Pages 100 and 101: Santa Fe Trail Center, Larned, KS; special thanks to Betsy Crawford-Gore, curator

*(continued on page 144)*

**SPECIAL PHOTOGRAPHY** (continued)

Page 100: Scotts Bluff National Monument; reproduction of *Westward America*, by William Henry Jackson

Pages 110 and 111: Tawantinsuyo Explorations, LLC, Boulder, CO; special thanks to Kevin Height

Pages 120 and 121 (except color photos on each page): Blue Ridge Parkway, Asheville, NC; special thanks to Jackie Holt for her assistance

Page 136 (bottom): Grace Cathedral, San Francisco, CA

**SPECIAL THANKS TO THOSE WHO ALLOWED US TO PHOTOGRAPH THEIR PATHS AND THEIR SUPPLIES:**

Jesse Israel and Sons Garden Center, Asheville, NC

J. Dabney Peeples Design Studio Display Gardens, Easley, SC (The talented team here was immensely helpful in many ways.)

J R Stone Sales Inc., Asheville, NC

The Home Depot, Asheville, NC

Turf Mountain Sod Inc., Hendersonville, NC

UNCA Botanical Gardens, Asheville, NC

Helga and Jack Beam residence, Asheville, NC

Brown residence, Greenville, SC

Clarkson residence, Easley, SC

Gannon residence, Greenville, SC

Graham A. Kimak residence, Greenville, SC

David and Deborah Lichtenfelt residence, Greenville, SC

Little residence, Greenville, SC

Mary McKinney residence, Greenville, SC

Morton residence, Greenville, SC

Glenn and Jan Spears residence, Greenville, SC

Wallenborn residence, Asheville, NC

Williams residence, Greenville, SC

The quotations on pages 9, 23, 39, 45, 61, and 127 were reprinted by permission; quotations on pages 7, and 15 are in the public domain.

# INDEX

# MAKING PATHS & WALKWAYS